"This book helps women to order their inner lives. It's a very useful tool for guiding women through a process of unpacking their beliefs about their identity and faith in Jesus Christ. I couldn't put it down, nor could I stop praying at the end."
—DR. SARAH SUMNER, associate professor, Ministry and Theology, Azusa Pacific University

The Intentional Woman will empower women by giving them tools under the guidance of the Holy Spirit to make intentional choices for purposeful living. This book has a broad appeal that every woman should process, no matter her family dynamic or career focus. The purpose of her life story will emerge with greater impact in her world."
—BEV HISLOP, faculty and director, Women's Center for Ministry, Western Seminary

The Intentional Woman is a transformational challenge for any woman desiring significant change in her life. It is a definitive guide that teaches how to live a more purposeful life and utilize one's often buried giftedness."
—JIM SMOKE, author; speaker; life coach

"This book will equip you to move from where you are to where you want to be, especially if you don't know where you are or want to be! Carol and Joan have made this journey and God is using them to guide other women along the path to intentional living."
—DR. SANDRA D. WILSON, seminary professor; speaker; author of *Released From Shame*

"Everyone likes a good story and my friend Carol reveals that the best story may be locked right in your own life. If you'd like to know the power of the story that God is writing in you and through you, then this is a necessary read."
—DR. JOSEPH M. STOWELL, president, Moody Bible Institute

Carol Travilla and
Joan C. Webb

the Intentional Woman

A Guide to Experiencing the Power of Your Story

NAVPRESS

BRINGING TRUTH TO LIFE
P.O. Box 35001, Colorado Springs, Colorado 80935

OUR GUARANTEE TO YOU

We believe so strongly in the message of our books that we are making this quality guarantee to you. If for any reason you are disappointed with the content of this book, return the title page to us with your name and address and we will refund to you the list price of the book. To help us serve you better, please briefly describe why you were disappointed. Mail your refund request to: NavPress, P.O. Box 35002, Colorado Springs, CO 80935.

The Navigators is an international Christian organization. Our mission is to reach, disciple, and equip people to know Christ and to make Him known through successive generations. We envision multitudes of diverse people in the United States and every other nation who have a passionate love for Christ, live a lifestyle of sharing Christ's love, and multiply spiritual laborers among those without Christ.

NavPress is the publishing ministry of The Navigators. NavPress publications help believers learn biblical truth and apply what they learn to their lives and ministries. Our mission is to stimulate spiritual formation among our readers.

Cover design by Dan Jamison
Cover illustration by Greg Hargreaves / Artville
Creative Team: Don Simpson, Karen Lee-Thorp, Vicki Witte, Darla Hightower, Glynese Northam

Some of the anecdotal illustrations in this book are true to life and are included with the permission of the persons involved. All other illustrations are composites of real situations, and any resemblance to people living or dead is coincidental.

Unless otherwise identified, all Scripture quotations in this publication are taken from the *HOLY BIBLE: NEW INTERNATIONAL VERSION*® (NIV®). Copyright © 1973, 1978, 1984 by International Bible Society. Used by permission of Zondervan Publishing House. All rights reserved. Other versions used include: *The Message: New Testament with Psalms and Proverbs* (MSG) by Eugene H. Peterson, copyright © 1993, 1994, 1995, used by permission of NavPress Publishing Group; the *New American Standard Bible* (NASB), © The Lockman Foundation 1960, 1962, 1963, 1968, 1971, 1972, 1973, 1975, 1977; the *Holy Bible, New Living Translation*, (NLT) copyright © 1996. Used by permission of Tyndale House Publishers, Inc., Wheaton, Illinois 60189. All rights reserved; and *The Living Bible* (TLB), copyright © 1971, used by permission of Tyndale House Publishers, Inc., Wheaton, IL 60189, all rights reserved.

Printed in the United States of America

1 2 3 4 5 6 7 8 9 10 / 05 04 03 02

FOR A FREE CATALOG OF
NAVPRESS BOOKS & BIBLE STUDIES,
CALL 1-800-366-7788 (USA)
OR 1-416-499-4615 (CANADA)

Dedication

We lovingly dedicate this book
to our daughters, Karen and Lynnette, and daughters-in-law, Jill and Anne.
You are intentional women with hearts for God.
You bring joy and love into our lives.
We feel blessed.

Table of Contents

Appreciation

The possibility for this book began that day we met for lunch in 1988. Our common desire to share how God has worked in our lives fueled our friendship. God has repeatedly surprised us by giving us opportunities to work together. Along the way God brought men and women into our lives who have supported us, believed in us, and prayed for us.

First we thank our loving and patient husbands, Ken and Richard. They have gone the extra mile supporting us in practical ways such as running errands, grocery shopping, providing meals, praying, and giving us freedom to complete this project.

Thank you to our friends, our LifePlan and coaching clients, the women in our workshops, and all the intentional women who gave us permission to share their powerful stories. You are too numerous to mention by name. Yet we want you to know that your encouragement and prayers have inspired us and kept us going.

Also we thank the capable team at NavPress that has guided us through this writing and publishing process.

Prep Steps

PART A:
HOW CAN I DISCOVER THE POWER OF MY LIFE STORY?

Key Verse: We pray for you all the time—pray that our God will make you fit for what he's called you to be, pray that he'll fill your good ideas and acts of faith with his own energy so that it all amounts to something.
(2 Thessalonians 1:11, MSG)

Living Intentionally

If I live intentionally, being true to my own personality, serving out of my God-given giftedness and calling, I no longer feel a need to envy anyone else's career, marriage, ministry, talents, or mission.

The day I (Joan) jotted these liberating words into my journal, I sighed with relief. I was forty years old. Believing this truth gradually changed my life. Although I rarely voiced envy, I was secretly disappointed that others had fulfilled their dreams but I had not. I longed to live out the purposes and desires that God had planted deep within my heart. Yet I was afraid.

Would God (and others) think I was selfish if I took the time to nurture my interests and gifts? Could God use my past experiences and accomplishments (even though some were not what I had wanted to do) to help me determine how to live more effectively today? Could I be certain that it was God who was encouraging me to make changes in my life?

During this questioning time in my life I watched Carol Travilla teach a Sunday school class at Wooddale Church in Eden Prairie, Minnesota. I stepped beyond my apprehension about what she might think of me and telephoned her, asking her to meet me for lunch. She agreed. Although she did not know me, she listened intently to my story. I told her about my recent decision to walk away from my business and shared how burnout had left me feeling empty and confused. I shared my desire to escape from the people-pleasing and action-obsessed lifestyle that was so familiar to me. I told her that I wanted to live for God—courageously and intentionally.

FRIENDS MENTORING FRIENDS

Several days later Carol telephoned to ask me to do some interior design work at her office. Our relationship began. As weeks turned into months and years, I learned that Carol had experienced difficult growing times, also. She identified with my passion to live "on-purpose" for God. Our connection grew into a friendship that Carol describes as "iron sharpening iron." We have a stimulating, motivating effect on one another. Carol is an extrovert, energized by interaction with others. I am an introvert, gaining strength and vitality from my alone times. We mentor and sharpen one another and therefore have become wiser, more intentional women.

We believe women can help each other develop into the persons God designed them to be. We have witnessed and experienced this exciting mentoring phenomenon in our own relationship and in the relationships of other women. We have come to understand that many women want to learn, share, and live intentionally, but feel too busy with their jobs, families, homes, church, and volunteer work to become involved in programs to develop lengthy life-purpose plans.

> *As iron sharpens iron, a friend sharpens a friend.*
>
> (Proverbs 27:17, NLT)

A REUSABLE FIVE-STEP PROCESS

In response to this obvious need, we have developed a process for helping one another learn to live meaningful, intentional, and God-honoring lives. You now hold this process tool in your hands. We hope to reduce the mystery and intimidation that often accompany trying to determine what to do with your life. Our interactive workbook offers you an inviting, practical, and reusable five-step method for:

- Recognizing the power of your personal life story and God's goodness in developing your story
- Discovering a next-step action focus for intentional living right now—in your current life stage

You may have the desire and time to delve more deeply into the topic of designing your personal life goals. If so, you may use this workbook in conjunction with other helpful manuals and technical books on the subject.

We wish we could share with each of you personally, but because that is impossible, we designed a way for us to work together. In the pages of this interactive workbook we share our own experiences, as well as the stories of friends. We will guide you as you gain clarification about:

- Who you are now: your present roles, temperament, and life stage.
- Where you have been: your past experiences and accomplishments.
- How knowing who you are and where you have been helps you experience the power of your life story, develop a current life focus, and become intentional about your personal and spiritual growth.
- How learning to appreciate God's goodness in producing your unique life script can help you love Him more.

It is our prayer that you will find joy and direction for living intentionally at each season of your life.

What to Expect

Each time you complete the exercises in this workbook, you will gain new insight about your current life stage and help in making wise choices for right now. There is no limit to the number of times you can work through this process. Here's what you can expect to do as you work through this reusable five-step process:

STEP ONE: COME AS YOU ARE TODAY

In this step, you will complete exercises that help you answer the following questions:

- What is good about my life today?
- What concerns me about my life right now?
- What is lacking in my life?
- How do I want God to help me?

STEP TWO: CELEBRATE YOUR YESTERDAYS

In step two, you will complete exercises that help you answer these questions:

- Is there power in *my* life story?
- What have I enjoyed throughout my life?
- Who has influenced me during my life?
- How have my past experiences shaped me?

STEP THREE: COMMIT IT ALL TO GOD

In this step, you will complete exercises that help you answer these questions:

- What are my unique characteristics and preferences?
- What is God teaching me about myself?
- How can I commit it all to God?

STEP FOUR: CONSIDER YOUR CHOICES

In step four, you will complete exercises that help you answer these questions:

- What are my opportunities and options?
- What are my current roles?
- What are my unique stressors and supports?

STEP FIVE: CLARIFY YOUR NEXT STEPS

In the final step of this process, you will answer these questions:

- What holds me back?
- How can I join God in living out of the power of my life story?
- What action step will I take?

Committing to one action step at a time leads to an entire lifetime of purposeful living. It helps you take personal responsibility for your own growth and assists you in deciding how to spend your time and energy right now.

Throughout this workbook, each time you are asked to finish a sentence, respond to a question, or complete an exercise, you will see the following symbol: ✍

✍ 1. As you anticipate working through these steps, begin by completing this sentence: I am interested in becoming focused and intentional because. . .

✍ 2. Complete this sentence: At this stage in my life, I look forward to. . .

Lifelong Adventure

We suggest that you ask another woman to join you in experiencing this five-step method for becoming an intentional woman who lives out of the power of her story. You might meet for breakfast (before work) or during your lunch hour to share your answers and inspiration. Or you could start a women's focus group at your church, with your neighbors, or with the mothers of your child's classmates. If it's impossible to meet face-to-face, you might consider doing the exercises on your own and then connecting for interaction with another woman on the telephone or via e-mail.

We have designed the exercises and tools in this workbook to be flexible. Perhaps you or your group would like to do one step per week for a six-week study. Or maybe you would like to use the book in a Sunday school class or weeknight setting. In this case, you may wish to spend two weeks on each step, making it a twelve-week program. Or you and your friends might choose to do all the steps during a weekend retreat. We encourage you to come just as you are today and join us on this lifelong adventure of becoming an intentional woman.

If you're using this workbook on your own, you're still not alone. Throughout the book you'll find boxes containing the real-life IW (Intentional Woman) stories of others who are traveling with you on this road.

*P*ART *B:*
WHAT IS INTENTIONAL LIVING, ANYWAY?

"I feel so unfocused and disorganized!" said Laura. She had just been downsized from her job, moved to a new city, and was trying to decide whether to get married again. "How can I manage all this change in my life and still commit to a new relationship?" she asked. "It's hard for me to be intentional. I wonder what in the world that is, anyway."

Perhaps, like Laura, you wonder what we mean by the term "intentional woman." An intentional woman works at becoming proactive instead of just letting life happen to her. The opposite of being intentional is being haphazard or purposeless about your thoughts, decisions, and actions—merely *reacting* to life's unexpected circumstances.

> *For a doubtful mind is as unsettled as a wave of the sea that is driven and tossed by the wind. People like that should not expect to receive anything from the Lord. They can't make up their minds. They waver back and forth in everything they do.*
>
> (James 1:6-8, NLT)

The intentional woman with a heart for God has a sense of God's purpose for her and is living true to her personality and giftedness. She accepts what she cannot change about her season and circumstances, making courageous and deliberate decisions about the things she can change. She is not self-absorbed to the point of leaving others out of her life, nor does she live her life through or for others. The attitudes and pressures of other people do not unduly influence her. She is focused and directed, not floundering or driven.

Because today's Christian woman is too busy just to keep adding to her already overwhelming to-do list, it's understandable that she might ask the questions, *Why should I spend energy trying to live intentionally? Why is it important for a woman to clarify her aspirations, discover and develop her God-given abilities, and make intentional plans about her next steps?*

The Key Reason for Living Intentionally

The key reason for living intentionally is to glorify God as the person He created you to be. In honoring your uniqueness, you come before your Creator and Savior with freedom and integrity. When I (Carol) was a child, I remember being taught that the "chief end of man" is to glorify God and enjoy Him forever. I sensed that my Sunday school teachers thought this was an important principle, yet it was confusing to me. What did they mean? And how was I supposed to accomplish this directive?

The Scotch catechism says that man's chief end is "to glorify God and enjoy Him forever." But we shall then know that these are the same thing. Fully to enjoy is to glorify. In commanding us to glorify Him, God is inviting us to enjoy Him.

(C. S. Lewis)

As I matured in my faith, I realized these instructors were trying to tell me that the ultimate purpose of every human being—man, woman, or child—is to praise and honor God with the life he or she is given. Gradually, this principle made more sense to me. It meant accepting my uniqueness—the way God created me—and pulling out all the stops to develop my gifts and use them deliberately to serve God here on earth.

Integrity grows as you allow God to guide you in becoming more honest with yourself, others, and God. Then you can live each new day to enjoy, honor, and worship God as the person He designed you to be.

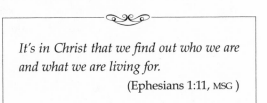

It's in Christ that we find out who we are and what we are living for.

(Ephesians 1:11, MSG)

Four Benefits of Living Intentionally

BENEFIT ONE: DEVELOP CONFIDENCE AND SELF-RESPECT.
Many women long to connect with their possibilities. Because you are reading this book, you are probably one of these women. God created you with unique temperament traits,

interests, and gifts. You have past experiences and potential accomplishments like no one else.

As you cooperate with God and accept responsibility for your adult choices, emotions, and behavior, you take positive steps toward living intentionally. Once you believe that you can change the things about your life over which you have control—in addition to accepting the things you cannot change—you are on the way to increasing self-respect. You gain renewed self-worth when you stop blaming your circumstances, family, or friends and start making on-purpose decisions about your immediate and long-range future. When you stay committed to the lifelong pursuit of knowing God and yourself better, you can enter each new day with confidence.

IW STORY: FOCUSING MY ENERGY

When I was young, I assumed I had unlimited energy. I could work all day and into the night, get a few hours of rest, and be ready to start again the next morning. Then one day, I came to the end of my strength. I learned a valuable lesson. Energy is *not* unlimited.

I needed to make some important choices about where to focus my energy. I noticed that my energy dissipated when I felt conflicted about what I was doing. So I began to prioritize my activities. I searched the Scripture for my own set of basic values. These values became a steadying influence for me when making choices.

To me, living intentionally means clinging tenaciously to these three primary concepts:

- My energy is limited, therefore I must focus.
- I can focus my energy by concentrating on the personal values I have chosen from Scripture.
- My focused energy powerfully fuels my consistent daily choices, so that I can live intentionally.

HOLLY DELHOUSAYE, FOUNDER OF
PRICKLY PERSPECTIVES

BENEFIT TWO: GAIN FOCUS AND DIRECTION.

I (Carol) felt anxious and overwhelmed until I understood the positive aspects of my high-energy and divergent (scattered) way of thinking and living. I felt I was not good enough, not organized enough, and never

> *My business is not to remake myself, but make the absolute best of what God made.*
> (Robert Browning)

accomplished enough. When I began to appreciate and accept my fun-loving, people-oriented personality, I gained focus and purpose. I became intentional about using my style to glorify God and serve others.

BENEFIT THREE: CONCENTRATE ON GOD'S IDEA FOR ME, NOT SOMEONE ELSE'S.

It's important for a woman to discover who God created her to *be*, and consequently, what He designed her to *do*, because if she doesn't learn and act on that knowledge, then she will probably end up living someone else's intent for her. It might please the other person, but it will leave her feeling restless, dull, and unfulfilled—disconnected from herself and maybe even from God.

It is sad when we women think and behave as though God's creative idea for us is not enough. We can become more influenced by what another person thinks or wants than by what God purposed. The subtle message is, *God, You must be wrong about this. I just can't trust You to do what is best for me.*

A woman who lives to please another person may think she has valid reasons for doing so. I (Joan) certainly did. One of my motives for living this way was that I thought God wanted this from me. I read the Bible and knew it directed me to be loving, kind, accepting, and giving. I wanted to obey the Golden Rule: Do unto others as you would have them do unto you. (See Matthew 7:12.) I did not want to act selfishly or appear unloving. So I hid what I liked, what I really wanted, and what I believed to be right for me when it did not coincide with my husband's ideas.

> *Once you accept responsibility for yourself, other people are powerless to impose their agendas and expectations on you. That is freedom and power. Freedom to choose consistent with your purpose.*
>
> (Kevin W. McCarthy, *The On-Purpose Person: Make Your Life Make Sense*)

BENEFIT FOUR: AVOID BURNOUT.

Eventually, this way of life led me into burnout. I felt dead inside. Still, I tried so hard to make everyone happy. I wanted to please God, but my actions proved that someone else was more important to me than God.

I slipped deeper into depression, overwork, and exhaustion until I reluctantly admitted, "I do not want to live this way any longer." Although uncertain about just what to do, I began to be honest with God about my thoughts, emotions, and needs. In turn, God slowly started revealing myself to me. I found I had some misconstrued ideas about how to be a loving and giving person. For the sake of peace I had ignored what God had showed me about myself and instead had adopted my mate's concept for me. I ended up where I didn't want to be.

It startled me to realize that someone else's opinion and agenda pulled more weight with me than God's did. I was hurt and sad that I had unintentionally treated God so poorly. However, my genuine pain gave me the motivation and courage I

> *You are either living your mission or you are living someone else's. Which shall it be?*
> (Laurie Beth Jones, *The Path*)

needed to change my direction and pursue God's intention for me. This is what He had wanted from me all along.

A BIBLICAL EXAMPLE: PETER'S PURPOSE

We can avoid burnout by focusing on God's purpose for us as individuals. Jesus' interaction with Peter helps us understand this truth.

1. Read John 21:17-21 (printed here). In the third paragraph of this passage, what did Jesus ask Peter to do?

2. What was Peter's final response to Jesus in the last paragraph?

> *The third time he said to him, "Simon son of John, do you love me?"*
>
> *Peter was hurt because Jesus asked him the third time, "Do you love me?" He said, "Lord, you know all things; you know that I love you."*
>
> *Jesus said, "Feed my sheep. I tell you the truth, when you were younger you dressed yourself and went where you wanted; but when you are old you will stretch out your hands, and someone else will dress you and lead you where you do not want to go." Jesus said this to indicate the kind of death by which Peter would glorify God. Then he said to him, "Follow me!"*
>
> *Peter turned and saw that the disciple whom Jesus loved was following them. (This was the one who had leaned back against Jesus at the supper and had said, "Lord, who is going to betray you?") When Peter saw him, he asked, "Lord, what about him?"*
>
> (John 21:17-21)

Jesus cooked breakfast for Peter, James, John, and a few other disciples. After they finished eating, Jesus started a one-on-one conversation with Peter. "Peter, do you care about me more than all the other important things in your life?" asked Jesus.

"Oh, yes, Lord," answered Peter. "You know I do."

"I have a special plan and purpose for you, Peter," continued Jesus. "I'm calling you to supervise, guide, and nurture those who choose to believe in Me after I'm gone."

Jesus based this calling for Peter on several factors: Peter's temperament, who God had created him to be, Peter's past experiences, and what Peter had learned about his own accomplishments and weaknesses. Jesus delivered a multifaceted life direction for a uniquely created person to be lived out to the glory of God and the good of others. Jesus gave Peter an awesome life mission. It fit him perfectly.

Yet, Peter's immediate response to this amazing and intimate moment with his Lord was: "But what is Your plan for him?" And Peter pointed toward his friend John.

Some of us, like Peter, are so concerned with how someone else is responding to God's call that we neglect to deal honestly with our own purpose from God. We actually honor Him when we allow Him to show us who we are and what we can become.

> *People who exercise their embryonic freedom day after day will, little by little, expand that freedom. People who do not will find that it withers until they are literally "being lived." They are acting out the scripts written by parents, associates, and society.*
>
> (Stephen R. Covey, *The 7 Habits of Highly Effective People*)

*L*IVING *I*NTENTIONALLY *M*EANS…

Becoming Free

You are personally responsible for who you are and what you decide before God. God doesn't expect you to make the spiritual or moral decisions for other people. Neither does God expect you to give up your own gifts, talents, personality, and heart passion just to please another. Placating another person (such as saying yes, no matter what you think or feel) seems like the unselfish thing to do because it brings an initial calm in the relationship. However, inauthentic harmony is not the kind of love God speaks about when He says to serve one another.

Accepting responsibility for your own choices, listening to what God has to say about you, and living out your own life purpose allows those around you to discover God's design for them. This freedom is one of the most significant gifts you can give those closest to you—the ones you influence daily. Then you and those you love can relax and enjoy serving God intentionally, each with your unique gifts and potential. This is God's plan. And it works.

> *For we are God's masterpiece. He has created us anew in Christ Jesus, so that we can do the good things he planned for us long ago.*
>
> (Ephesians 2:10, NLT)

3. Read Ephesians 2:10 (printed above). According to this verse, what does God have planned for you to do?

4. You are God's masterpiece. What does that mean to you?

5. Read Philippians 1:6 (printed here). Describe the work God has started in you.

> *Being confident of this, that he who began a good work in you will carry it on to completion until the day of Christ Jesus.*
>
> (Philippians 1:6)

6. How long will God continue to do a good work in and through you?

God is the most creative, capable, and committed artist you could ever imagine. He takes joy in painting masterpieces. You are His living masterpiece and He longs for you to cooperate with His ongoing creative work.

Accepting the Process

Living according to God's plan and purpose for you is an important key to glorifying God and enjoying Him forever. But it doesn't happen overnight. It is a step-by-step process.

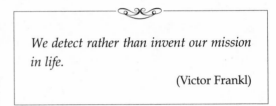

We detect rather than invent our mission in life.

(Victor Frankl)

Perhaps it puzzles you that you might need to address this purpose issue repeatedly. Like many women, perhaps you like to do something once, do it well, and move on to the next goal. However, if you can accept the fact that you will not be able to have your entire life mission and implementation strategy figured out perfectly, you can actually experience a sense of relief. God invites you to enjoy your journey with Him.

IW STORY: RELAXING WITH THE PROCESS

I was fifty-five years old, still struggling with what I wanted to be when I grew up, and feeling old and unusable. Then I sensed God urging me to go to back to school. I enrolled in a Master of Divinity program.

My focused and purposeful goal: To make rapid progress. At my age, I felt I couldn't waste any more time. I had always felt one step behind, learning today what I should have known years before. After reminding the Lord that I was older now and hopefully wiser, I asked Him to skip the baby steps and get on to the big stuff.

One day as I prayed, I thought, *What if Jesus had come with this hurry up attitude?* I envisioned Him saying to His Father, "OK, let's get busy. I have the whole world to save in just over three years. For starters, I'll need more than these twelve men." However, Jesus kept God's perspective. He stayed connected to His Father and accomplished everything that needed to be done.

I began to relax when I realized that my

Heavenly Father accepts and enjoys the process as well as the result. At one time, I felt I had wasted too many years by not recognizing my God-given purpose and pursuing it intentionally. But now I realize that God has been there all along, giving meaning to each of my life experiences.

REBECCA ANDERSON, STUDENT AT
PHOENIX SEMINARY

Reducing Confusion

"It is not so important to have the perfect mission statement," says Lynnette Rasmussen, with Summit Advantage Training and Coaching. "In fact, I encourage my clients not to wait for that moment [in order] to start living with direction. I like to think of it as having an overall umbrella of purpose for your life, so that you can walk forward intentionally. This umbrella helps you decide what to say no to and what to say yes to."

There are many worthwhile opportunities available to women today. It *is* confusing trying to decipher what to do. However, by choosing to live within the guidelines of your unique God-given design and purpose, you can make more reasonable yes and no decisions.

MOVING ON

The primary reason for intentional living is to glorify God as the person He intended you to be and to live out the good deeds He planned for you to do. In addition, living intentionally helps you:

- Reduce stress and daily anxiety
- Develop confidence and self-respect
- Gain direction for making decisions
- Establish healthy relationships
- Avoid burnout

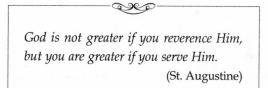

God is not greater if you reverence Him, but you are greater if you serve Him.

(St. Augustine)

7. Which benefit of intentional living interests you right now?

"My purpose is to give life in all its fullness."

(John 10:10, NLT)

8. What can you do during this next week to remind yourself that you want to experience this benefit?

This adventure starts where you are *today*. Reading and completing the exercises in step one will help you understand your current life situation—your reality, needs, and desires. You might discover you would like more space for answering the questions or completing the exercises in this workbook. If so, we suggest you keep an Intentional Woman notebook or journal to record your additional thoughts and insights.

Step One: Come as You Are Today

PART A:
WHERE AM I RIGHT NOW?

❧

Key Verse: The LORD says, "I will guide you along the best pathway for your life. I will advise you and watch over you." (Psalm 32:8, NLT)

God's Promise to Guide

I (Carol) was a nineteen-year-old college student, struggling with what classes to take, who to be, and what to do with the rest of my life. I felt disoriented and alone. One weekend I went home to visit, and during a meeting at my home church, a friend's father gave a short testimony. He quoted Psalm 32:8, and immediately I claimed it as my special promise from God. I sensed God saying, "Carol, I will teach you. I will help you with what to do with your life. Watch me. I will guide you with my eye."

Through the following years when I had no idea which way to turn, I believed the promise in Psalm 32:8. God assured me that He would instruct me and help me with my decisions. The phrase in the Bible version I read—"I will guide you with My eye"—fascinated me. Gradually, I realized that although God said He would watch over me, I could not decipher what He wanted me to do unless I kept my eye on Him. How could He show me anything or direct me about my future if I was not looking at Him?

I have learned the value of focusing on the Lord through prayer and Bible reading—depending on His Spirit for insight, courage, and power to act on what I learn. Even today, after the decades of many moves, blessings, and disappointments, this special verse remains God's distinct assurance to me. We have chosen Psalm 32:8 as our key verse for the first step in this process of becoming an intentional woman.

1. Read Psalm 32:8 (printed on page 25). Using your own words, rewrite this verse as if God were speaking it directly to you.

As He has done for me (Carol), God longs to protect and guide you. He wants to help you make wise decisions in the midst of your sometimes confusing circumstances and busy schedules.

Finding Balance

Airplanes, fax machines, microwaves, cell telephones, and computers encourage us to hurry up and accomplish more. How can we find a wise balance in this frantic world?

> *So whether you eat or drink or whatever you do, do it all for the glory of God.*
> (1 Corinthians 10:31)

Deciding what you want most from life and weeding out activities that detract from your goals will help you feel more balanced. Our Creator gives you one earthly life. He doesn't push you to fill every moment of your life with planned activity or service. God is happy for you to slow down in order to determine where you want to go, what you want to do, and who you want to be. He wants—even expects—you to take responsibility for each area of your life.

Yet perhaps you've been conditioned to believe that God is not concerned with certain areas, so you should not be, either. Maybe you talk with Him about your spiritual needs and goals but minimize your other needs.

2. Read Luke 2:52 (printed here). Why do you think this verse is included in the Bible?

> *And Jesus grew in wisdom and stature, and in favor with God and men.*
> (Luke 2:52)

Jesus grew relationally, physically, and spiritually. He also developed prudence in handling life's varied circumstances. By His Son's example, God affirms that He is interested and concerned with the total person. He wants all His children to be balanced individuals, continually maturing in every way.

> *Just as nature needs balance, people need balance. We need time to be whole persons, and this means balance.*
>
> (Anne Wilson Schaef, *Meditations for Women Who Do Too Much*)

The next exercise is designed to help you gain a clearer picture of where you are right now—not yesterday—but *today* as you face tomorrow. Maybe the concerns and duties of one life area are overpowering the other areas. Getting an overall view of your life can help you identify the areas that need specific attention. Then you can make adjustments to regain balance.

Balance itself has no specific objective. It is a constant state of motion. To help understand this, imagine that you have just completed the following exercise:

- You stood up and twirled around several times.
- You ran in place for several minutes and skipped to the corner of the room and back.
- You twirled around twice more.
- Then you immediately tried to balance on one foot.

Imagine the subtle adjustments you had to make in your foot and body to maintain equilibrium. This imaginary activity is designed to give you a picture of what you are attempting to do in balancing the different aspects and roles of your life during any given day. Developing balance is a skill.

> *From time to time, On-Purpose Persons may choose to be out of balance. Perhaps there's a major project that's essential to our purpose—then we go out of balance on a temporary basis. Giving ourselves consent to be off-balance tempers the ideal with the real—life, after all has surprises. A few words of caution are appropriate: Constant out-of-balance activity leads to being off-purpose.*
>
> (Kevin W. McCarthy, *The On-Purpose Person: Making Your Life Make Sense*)

Wheel of Life

To help you assess your life as a whole and see which areas are currently out of balance, we offer the Wheel of Life inventory exercise. The Wheel assesses eight areas of your life.

- Fun and Recreation (time-out, hobbies, exploring, re-creation)
- Self-care (physical well-being, health issues, exercise, soul-care, journaling)
- Finances (stewardship and money management)

- Life Work (vocation, career—including full-time mother or homemaker)
- Family Life (children, in-laws, grandchildren, extended family)
- Marriage/Romance (spouse, dating)
- Friends/Relationships (neighbors, coworkers, friends, fellow church members)
- Spiritual Life (faith, relationship with God, service, church work)

The Wheel of Life tool registers your perceptions of your current satisfaction in each of the eight areas of your life. As you contemplate your satisfaction level in each life area, you may encounter some surprises—or confusion. You might be a single woman and have little romance in your life right now, yet you are satisfied with that. Consider this when you mark your wheel. Or perhaps you just left a job and have not started a new position yet, but you are

> *Much of the dissatisfaction among Christian women today is, I believe, due to our choosing God as the center of our lives (being) but not lining up with the purposes God has put within us (doing).*
>
> (Jan Johnson, *Living a Purpose-Full Life*)

pleased with your situation. Maybe you quit your outside job to stay home with your new baby and this decision necessitated a reduction in your family budget, but you are content with that reality. Perhaps you have a chronic medical condition but have learned good coping skills and are pleased with your situation at the current time. In that case, you would register your physical well-being with a higher number than one might expect. Resist completing your wheel according to how you think someone else might register your level of satisfaction.

3. With the center of the wheel as 0 and the outer edge as 10, rank your *level of satisfaction* with each life area by drawing a curved line to create a new outer edge (see example). The new perimeter of the circle represents your Wheel of Life.

How Bumpy Is My Ride?

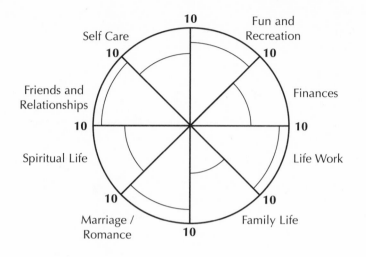

EXAMPLE

The eight sections in the Wheel of Life represent eight areas of your daily life. Look over the example and then complete your wheel.

MY WHEEL

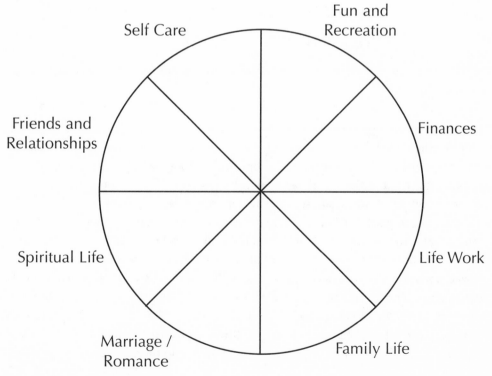

4. How bumpy would your ride be if this were a real wheel?

5. What is one thing you learned from your Wheel of Life inventory?

No Perfect Wheel

When I (Joan) first drew my wheel, it represented how bumpy my life was at the time. The second time I did it, there was not such a huge disparity between each area. The one who guided me through this exercise said the objective was not necessarily to have all 9s or 10s. The aim was to gain a visual aid that would assist me in making choices that lead to a more satisfied life. She assured me that I could have all 7s and 8s and still feel balanced.

We're unlikely to have all 10s all the time because life here on this earth will never be perfect and our lives are in a constant state of flux. Any time you feel overwhelmed, this simple exercise can help you evaluate your life situation and make adjustments to raise your satisfaction level. It gives you a base from which to work, helping you make proactive decisions instead of just letting life happen to you. Often, when you make necessary changes in one aspect of your life, it positively affects the other areas and raises your overall satisfaction level.

IW STORY: COURAGE TO BE INTENTIONAL

As soon as I was given the instructions for doing the Wheel of Life inventory tool, I knew right away there would be at least one area that I would register a low number and make my wheel of life very lopsided.

Consequently, I considered fudging a little to make it appear more in balance. After all, I reasoned, no one would know. I wanted to look good to my new friends. However, I also knew that I wanted to gain as much as I could from this IW process, so I concluded that I would be honest.

Then I faced an entirely different dilemma. Being honest about my current dissatisfaction in these life areas meant I would be faced with the need to take stock and *do* something tangible so I would not feel so out of balance.

AUDREY THORKELSON,
LEADERSHIP TRAINER

IW STORY: I CAN DO THAT!

I marked each spoke of the Wheel of Life with an 8, 9, or 10 and felt pleased. However, when I came to the Self Care area, I said, "I marked it a 5, because I have Chronic Fatigue Syndrome and there is nothing I can do about it." Another area was lower also, so my friend and I discussed ways to raise my satisfaction level there. I committed to begin working on it the next day. Then we went back to the Self Care area. She said, "What could you do to raise the 5 to a 6?"

"Don't have time to exercise right now," I answered. "But maybe I could go to sleep fifteen minutes earlier each night. Yes, I can do that."

"Will doing that change your 5 to a 6?" asked my friend.

"Yes, it will," I admitted with surprise. Then I realized that my "there is nothing I can do about it" comment was not entirely honest. I acknowledge my medical problems are ongoing. Yet, I now know (more fully than before) that I do have options and choices even in these areas where I thought I had no control.

LYNN SMITH (NAME CHANGED),
WORKING WIFE AND MOTHER

Part B:
WHAT IS GOING ON IN MY LIFE?

What Is Good about My Life Today?

Recently, when I (Carol) paused to answer the question *What is good about my life right now?* I realized anew how my life is filled with many positive circumstances.

- I am experiencing the results of consistently working through the five steps we recommend in this book.
- I do a better job of accepting my limitations and strengths now.
- I have developed a more contented heart since I began to understand the importance of having realistic expectations in each area of my life.
- I have a solid marriage. I feel I have been blessed by having a mate like my husband, Ken. He values glorifying God with his uniqueness, too. Still, it hasn't always been smooth sailing. Early in our marriage I depended on Ken to meet all my intimacy needs. I now know that this is impossible for any human being to do.
- I have wonderful children, grandchildren, and extended family. I enjoy living near some of my family.
- My work as a LifePlan facilitator is rewarding.
- Through the years in ministry and business, I have developed a strong network of caring friends and colleagues.

I am pleased with what I call my personal capital account. You have such an account as well. The assets in your account may include your history, abilities, gifts, pain, forgiven sins, accomplishments, friendships, family, network, spiritual growth, and reputation.

1. To help you determine what is in your personal capital account, answer this question: *What is good about my life right now?*

I have the privilege and opportunity to optimize my personal capital.

What Concerns Me about My Life Right Now?

Some of you may have current life concerns that include dealing with life-threatening illnesses, divorce, difficult children, financial loss, singleness, or career disappointment. Your concerns will vary depending on your season and current circumstances. This exercise is geared to help you be realistic about your struggles and determine what is troubling you today.

A continual concern for me (Carol) is how to maintain my health, which has been a lifelong roller coaster experience. I struggle staying committed to living a balanced life. I have a tendency to overdo as soon as I feel good physically.

Also, I have noticed that with each passing year I gain more relationships. For example, I gain more family members as relatives marry and have children. Also, as I meet new friends and clients, I still want to

> *Honor your feelings. They tell the truth about how you really experience the world. No one really benefits from your pretending. You can only see others as clearly as you see yourself.*
>
> (Stephen C. Paul, *Illuminations: Visions for Change, Growth and Self-Acceptance*)

remain in contact with my former associates and friends. Consequently, another concern is that I will be wise about knowing what to subtract so that I can experience the blessings that come with each new season of my life.

2. To help you determine what has a tendency to preoccupy your thoughts right now, answer the question, *What concerns me about my life at the current time?*

> *My concerns are an opportunity to identify focus for growth.*

What Is Lacking in My Life Right Now?

When your job, environment, or a relationship changes, or you feel restless and confused about a situation, pause to answer this question: *What is lacking in my life right now?* Stay quiet long enough to recognize your honest responses. These responses can help you recognize potential solutions for filling the voids in your life.

For example, a while back, I (Carol) asked myself, *What is lacking in my life right now?* I realized I lacked a sense of teamwork. I missed working with the staff at my clinic in Minnesota. Since moving to Arizona, I have worked from my home office and at times felt isolated.

I knew I could not go back to the previous way I worked. Still, I realized I had the opportunity to fill the void in a different way. I talked with God about my desire and considered my options. As a result, during the last year I have become more involved with the women on the ministry team at church. Then God surprised me by moving Joan here to Arizona from Minnesota. We have the opportunity to work together. I chuckle when I think about how different I feel now than I did before.

In fact, the other day as I was doing this exercise, I realized that a void in my life right now is "time-outs." I need some respite—time away for renewal. This is a void I can fill by saying no to a few requests and scheduling some alone time on my calendar.

3. To help determine what you are missing in your life, answer the question, *What is lacking in my life right now?*

> *Intentionality and self-discipline are crucial in implementing hoped-for changes.*
> (Jeannette Bakke, *Holy Invitations*)

You can work through these exercises again at different intervals in your life. Even next week you may respond differently to these three questions. These exercises take a snapshot of your life—at the moment.

IW STORY: I LIKE WHERE I AM RIGHT NOW

A little over a year ago, I was faced with the question, *What concerns me right now?* Immediately, I knew my major concern was my job. Every morning as I looked into the mirror, I saw a depressed woman staring back at me. Ironically, I enjoyed what I was doing. Yet for months I had been doubting my competency to do a job I had performed for over twenty years. My boss was—in the opinion of my friends—abusive. I felt trapped because my generous salary made it difficult for me to leave.

The answer to the question, *What is lacking in my life right now?* was obvious, also. *Joy.* My job was stealing the joy from my life. I was unhappy on the job, unhappy in the morning, in the evening, and on the weekend. *Christians are supposed to be filled with joy*, I thought. However, I felt dead inside and I just didn't care.

I knew that my concern about my job was an opportunity for me to make a decision that would enhance my growth and that my lack of joy was an invitation for me to fill the void. Still, it was difficult for me to make a move. Finally, after talking with friends and praying, I decided to resign. I grabbed what little courage I had left and answered job ads. The interview process renewed my confidence. Others *wanted* me to be part of their organization. By the end of February I had a nice job offer. Interestingly, when I told my employer, he created a different position for me in a more positive environment, so I stayed.

To the other question, *What is good about my life right now?* I can say that I now feel balanced and joyful. I am no longer overextending myself—for the sake of making peace at any cost. I can now say *no.* I no longer must be in a perpetual state of motion just to prove my value. I am learning that it is not what I *do* for God, but my *relationship* with Him that is most important. I like where I am right now.

JACKIE REED,
ADMINISTRATIVE ASSISTANT

The Good, the Concerns, and the Voids Overlap

While you were completing the Where Am I Right Now? exercise, you may have found that your responses overlapped. For example, I (Joan) can list the following good points about my life:

- I feel better since I discovered some treatments that help my fibromyalgia and menopausal symptoms.
- I have a loving husband, and we are learning to flex with the ongoing changes of our empty nest.
- I enjoy living near our son and daughter and their families.
- I delight in my new role as grandma to Annika and Max.
- I am fulfilling a ministry career dream through writing, coaching, and speaking.
- I live near Carol and we are able to work together.
- *And* after twenty years of experiencing cold winters, I now enjoy living where it's warm.

Some of my concerns are in direct relation to what is good in my life. We live in the Arizona warmth and sunshine now and I love it, but it was a major career shift that moved us here. With this change, I feel uncertain. I wonder what we will be doing this time next year and how the changes will affect us, our children, and my work.

The voids in my life seem to be a result of the uncertainties. In response to this question, *What are the voids in my life right now?* I listed the following:

- When we left Minnesota, I left several ministry connections, including the Bible study class I taught. Since moving, I need to make new connections.
- I miss my friend Sue. For ten years we studied and prayed together every Wednesday. Now we live almost 1,300 miles apart and I feel the loss.
- Previously I met with other writers regularly. I miss this critique group.
- When our family moved across the country, we downsized to one car. Although we have adjusted, I miss the freedom I felt when I could just "get up and go" without making prior arrangements.

> *There is as much guidance in what does not and cannot happen in my life as there is in what can and does—maybe more.*
>
> (Parker J. Palmer, *Let Your Life Speak: Listening for the Voice of Vocation*)

Partnering with God

Occasionally I get discouraged about the uncertainties that the concerns and voids bring. When I think about my past disappointments, I'm tempted to pretend that nothing is amiss or try to hide my feelings and thoughts. Then I remind myself that the areas of my perceived lack are opportunities for me to make choices that foster growth and propel me into new adventures with my heavenly Father.

"We don't give God a chance to do 'His thing' when we run away," says my friend Linda Linder, a women's Bible teacher from Edina, Minnesota. Perhaps your circumstances are not exactly as you envisioned they would be at this time in your life. Yet when you make an intentional decision to partner with God, you can be assured that He is in the process of fulfilling His commitment to guide and produce good in you.

You will take a major step in the right direction when you identify your emotions, thoughts, and needs. You have just answered questions about the good, the concerns, and the voids in your life. You may be experiencing mixed emotions such as frustration and hopefulness. Walking through the questioning and discouragement—instead of retreating—will reap worthwhile benefits. No matter what your feelings or thoughts right now, hang in there—the process *is* the journey.

The surest method of arriving at a knowledge of God's eternal purposes about us is to be found in the right use of the present moment. God's will does not come to us in the whole, but in fragments and generally in small fragments. It is our business to piece it together, and to live it as one orderly vocation.

(F. W. Faber)

*P*ART *E.*
HERE I AM, LORD.

Come near to God and he will come near to you.

James 4:8

Praying God's Words

Years ago, right before our family moved to Minnesota, I (Joan) read Psalm 27:4 during my alone time. My heart's desire was to know God intimately, to live in constant awareness of His presence, and to enjoy His friendship every day. So, I paraphrased the psalmist's words and prayed, *Lord, what I want most of all is the privilege of being with You every day of my life, delighting in who You are, and basking in Your majesty and greatness.*

As I wrote down this prayer in my journal, I sensed God urging me to read the next verse: "There I'll be when troubles come. He will hide me" (TLB). I really didn't want that part of the passage—with its hint of unpleasant things ahead—and told God so. Still, it seemed to me that God was prodding me to add it to my prayer. So I completed my above prayer with the following words: *When trouble comes, there I'll be, safe in Your presence.*

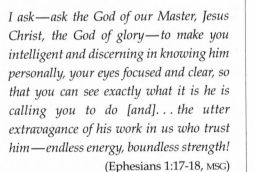

The one thing I ask of the LORD—
the thing I seek most—
is to live in the house of the LORD all the
days of my life,
delighting in the LORD's perfections
and meditating in his Temple.
(Psalm 27:4, NLT)

One week after we arrived in Minnesota (in weather that was 20 degrees *below* zero), I had premature labor pains, went into the hospital, and lost my baby. I was five months pregnant. It was a devastating time. My head felt like it was in a vice, yet I felt unexplainably safe. I had heard God's promise to me, prayed God's words back to Him, and relied on His trustworthy and loving character. He carried me through. In the midst of it all, I experienced the desire of my heart: to know God more intimately.

PRAYER PREPARES

The next exercise is designed to help you develop a practical prayer tool for getting to know God better as you learn who He designed you to be and what He wants you to do. This tool is similar to one that Joan introduced at a writing seminar that I (Carol) attended. I had been in private practice as a psychologist in Minnesota for ten years. I loved what I was doing, and my practice was successful.

Yet I felt restless and I couldn't understand why. *Do You want me to do something different, Lord? I hope You are not asking me to write. I really don't want to do that again.* I was attending Joan's writing seminar merely to encourage her. (I'm good at concentrating on someone else's needs rather than my own.)

Driving to the workshop, I had a thought—God-given, I now believe. *Carol, why don't you go for you?* My initial response was, *Go for me? Can't I just go to help her?* Finally, I decided to change my focus and go expecting to gain something for myself.

I ask—ask the God of our Master, Jesus Christ, the God of glory—to make you intelligent and discerning in knowing him personally, your eyes focused and clear, so that you can see exactly what it is he is calling you to do [and]. . . the utter extravagance of his work in us who trust him—endless energy, boundless strength!
(Ephesians 1:17-18, MSG)

In one session, Joan explained how to write a devotional from a Bible passage. As I skimmed the list of suggested Bible verses, I stopped on Isaiah 43:18-19: "Forget the former things; do not dwell on the past. See, I am doing a new thing! Now it springs up; do you not perceive it? I am making a way in the desert and streams in the wasteland."

Immediately I knew this verse was God's Word to me. However, the only part I really understood was the phrase "Do you not perceive it?" *No, Lord, I don't perceive it,* I wrote in my notes. *I only feel restlessness. What do you mean by "forget the former things"?* I asked God these questions repeatedly for the next few weeks.

Four months after that workshop, my husband, Ken, received a telephone call inviting him to join the pastoral staff of a church in Arizona. *Lord, I get it now. You are making a way in the desert—literally.* Saying yes to the move meant I had to forget the former things because my counseling licenses in Minnesota were not reciprocal in Arizona. I was faced with adjusting the mental and emotional picture I had of myself as a practicing psychologist, meeting with clients daily in my clinic. While I adjusted to the move, I often felt isolated and out of step. Gradually, I accepted that God was doing a completely new thing in my life, and in His great kindness, He had given me the verse in preparation.

My Personal Prayer

1. From the list of Scripture verses on pages 39-40, choose one or two that represent what you are asking God to do at this time or what you sense God is promising you. Then in the space provided, write your chosen verse or verses in the form of a prayer to God.

The one thing I ask of the LORD—
the thing I seek most—
is to live in the house of the LORD all the days of my life,
delighting in the LORD's perfections
and meditating in his Temple.
For he will conceal me there when troubles come;
he will hide me in his sanctuary.
(Psalm 27:4-5, NLT)

The LORD will fulfill his purpose for me; your love, O LORD, endures forever.
(Psalm 138:8)

Let the morning bring me word of your unfailing love, for I have put my trust in you. Show me the way I should go, for to you I lift up my soul.
(Psalm 143:8)

Trust in the LORD with all your heart and lean not on your own understanding; in all your ways acknowledge him, and he will make your paths straight.
(Proverbs 3:5-6)

"For I am the LORD, your God, who takes hold of your right hand and says to you, 'Do not fear; I will help you.'"   *(Isaiah 41:13)*

"I will lead the blind by ways they have not known, along unfamiliar paths I will guide them; I will turn the darkness into light before them and make the rough places smooth. These are the things I will do; I will not forsake them."
(Isaiah 42:16)

"Forget the former things; do not dwell on the past. See, I am doing a new thing! Now it springs up; do you not perceive it? I am making a way in the desert and streams in the wasteland."
(Isaiah 43:18-19)

"Come to me, all you who are weary and burdened, and I will give you rest."
(Matthew 11:28)

However, I consider my life worth nothing to me, if only I may finish the race and complete the task the Lord Jesus has given me.   *(Acts 20:24)*

Give yourselves completely to God since you have been given new life. And use your whole body as a tool to do what is right for the glory of God.
(Romans 6:13, NLT)

I am convinced that nothing can ever separate us from his love. Death can't, and life can't. The angels can't, and the demons can't. Our fears for today, our worries about tomorrow, and even the powers of hell can't keep God's love away. Whether we are high above the sky or in the deepest ocean, nothing in all creation will ever be able to separate us from the love of God that is revealed in Christ Jesus our Lord.
(Romans 8:38-39, NLT)

To this end I labor, struggling with all his energy, which so powerfully works in me.
(Colossians 1:29)

God doesn't want us to be shy with his gifts, but bold and loving and sensible.
(2 Timothy 1:7, MSG)

Therefore, since we are surrounded by such a great cloud of witnesses, let us throw off every-thing that hinders and the sin that so easily entangles, and let us run with perseverance the race marked out for us. (Hebrews 12:1)

Each one should use whatever gift he has received to serve others, faithfully administering God's grace in its various forms. (1 Peter 4:10)

Write your prayer here.

2. To what need in your life does this verse relate?

3. Write your prayer (or a phrase from it) on a sticky note and place it where you will notice it every day this week and remember to pray. (You might attach it to your computer, calendar, journal, bathroom mirror, or dashboard.) Where will you place your verse prayer?

IW STORY: COMFORT FROM GOD'S WORD

I had been happily married for thirty-seven years when my husband, Bob, collapsed with a massive fatal heart attack while entering church for the evening service. Shocked, I hoped I would die, too; but I didn't.

Bob had provided a sense of security for me. I always felt surrounded by a circle of love. I operated freely and confidently within that safe circle. After his death, I still had a good job, so managing finances wasn't a problem for me. But the loneliness was nearly unbearable.

I made an intentional decision to do the necessary work of grief. I reached out to others, attended workshops, searched the Bible for comfort, and continued my everyday ritual of going to my job in education. When my initial shock subsided, I organized grief groups at my church. I found great consolation in helping others. Yet I found my greatest solace in the Scriptures.

My friend Carol Travilla taught me to journal. When I read a Bible passage, I looked for a verse that had special meaning for me. In my journal I wrote the date and a prayer based on the verse, finishing with a statement of thanksgiving. I felt safe expressing my heartbreak on paper to God. Nine months after my husband's death, when my emotions were still raw, I wrote the following prayers:

JOURNAL ENTRY, SEPTEMBER 15
"But he took note of their distress when he heard their cry; for their sake he remembered his covenant and out of his great love he relented." (Psalm 106:44-45)

MY PRAYER: Lord, I am in distress. Forgive my impatience. Help me to learn what you have for me. I want to love others and to minister to them. This may be my happiness.

JOURNAL ENTRY, NOVEMBER 27
"If your law had not been my delight, I would have perished in my affliction." (Psalm 119:92)

Moving On

In step one, you completed exercises designed to help you:

- Become more aware of your current circumstances and how you think and feel about them.
- Identify areas where you want to make adjustments.
- Talk to God about what is happening in your life right now.

In the next section, you will gain perspective on your unique past and how God is using those experiences in your life now.

Step Two: Celebrate Your Yesterdays

PART A:
THERE'S POWER IN MY STORY?

Key Verse:
I trust in you, O LORD;
I say, "You are my God."
My times are in your hands;. . .
Let your face shine on your servant;
save me in your unfailing love.
(Psalm 31:14-16)

Joan's Story: The Off-Purpose Pitfall

About twenty-five years ago, I (Joan) scribbled the following words on a small piece of scrap paper and slid it into the pages of my Bible: *Lord, show me who I am now and who I can become—the person You had in mind when You created me.* Since then, I've written this simple, earnest prayer in my journal countless times.

In the following years, I enjoyed working in my business, but I really relished my studying, teaching, and writing ministry as a pastor's wife. Then suddenly I lost my platform for this beloved ministry when my husband changed careers. For seven years I lived in silent disappointment, pushing down my sadness and hurt. I fooled myself into thinking everything was fine. I coped and compensated by dedicating my energy and time to expanding my business. This worked. My sales and job success multiplied. My husband was proud of me and my accomplishments. His opinion meant a great deal to me—almost more than anything else.

Deep down I knew I was losing me, that *Joan* was slipping away. Still, I tried harder to do it all right. I said yes to more clients, working late many nights. I neglected my physical, social, and spiritual needs, concentrating on making everyone else happy. Eventually, I burned out. I had become *off purpose* with my true desires, hopes, and goals.

Because I found it difficult to think or feel, I functioned (especially with clients) by envisioning myself as a machine that I could turn off and on. When I was in my office, I felt like I was in a POW camp. I wanted to leave, but I didn't want to be a quitter. Finally, I summoned the courage to walk away from this business that I had grown from nothing to a million dollars in sales.

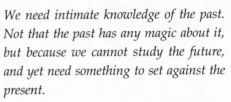

We need intimate knowledge of the past. Not that the past has any magic about it, but because we cannot study the future, and yet need something to set against the present.

(C. S. Lewis)

I knew I was in trouble on the inside, but I didn't know what to do about it. I felt angry, sad, and empty. The human being named Joan Carol Webb, with God-given gifts, talents, and dreams, was fried. I was terrified of rocking the boat and changing the way I related to my husband. I was afraid of backing away from my work. I was afraid of being rejected if I altered my attitudes about pleasing others.

In spite of the fear, I started taking baby steps toward finding me—the person God created. More than anything I wanted to live out my personal call from God. When I was in seventh grade, I said yes to God's call to live, work, and just *be* for Him. I really didn't doubt that call. But, at this time in my life, my circumstances were not conducive to living it out. So I lived off-purpose.

For God did not give us a spirit of timidity, but a spirit of power, of love and of self-discipline.

(2 Timothy 1:7)

FEAR RELEASED TO FAITH

My kids were growing up, and I grieved because I thought I hadn't directed or encouraged them the way I wanted to. I was getting older and didn't like who I had become. I was apprehensive about whether I'd make good use of my remaining time, because my mind couldn't hold a thought for very long, and my honest emotions had been ignored for so long that I scarcely felt. I knew God loved me, but I couldn't feel it. My husband said he loved me, yet I doubted that. I wondered if I would ever think and reason adequately again.

I sought the advice of a few wise people. We looked at the reasons I had allowed myself to get into this predicament. I admitted that

People are fond of saying that "the past is dead," but it is actually the future that is dead—and we make it come alive only by applying what we have learned from the living past to the present.

(Sydney Harris)

my rushaholic, people-pleasing, and everything-must-be-just-right behavior was obsessive and contributed to my unhealthy condition. I hated what I was discovering, yet at the same time, I sensed God wanted me to keep going on this unfamiliar and uncomfortable journey toward a renewed life.

Gradually, I decided I was not in such a hurry anymore. Because I couldn't figure it out, think it out, or perform it out, I figured all I could do was give each day to God—He was big enough to handle it.

I begged God for courage. Sometimes I felt so anxious that my body would shake as I attempted to fight off waves of nausea. I ached to be a writer, so one of the risks I took was to attend a Minnesota Christian Writers Guild meeting one Monday night. I walked into the meeting room and sat alone on the back row. I knew I couldn't change everything all at once, but this was one thing I could do.

I remember the days of long ago;
I meditate on all your works
and consider what your
hands have done.
I spread out my hands to you;
my soul thirsts for you like
a parched land.
(Psalm 143:5-6)

Several months later I drove to a local bookstore and bought the new Writer's Market Guide. I promptly put it into a paper bag to hide it. I didn't want anyone to see it and mock me.

Increasingly, my fear surrendered to faith as I took deliberate steps to stop hiding and live, regardless of anyone else's disapproval. During these years of change, growth, healing, and renewal, it dawned on me that God was in the process of answering my twenty-five-year-old prayer: *Lord, show me who I am now, and who I can become—the person You had in mind when You created me.*

Carol's Story: No Longer a Half Brick Short

"You know, Carol," explained my mother several years ago, "you were the child to save our marriage." At first the news shocked me. Yet, when I thought about it, I understood my childhood experiences better. My parents' marriage was chronically conflicted. As a child, I didn't understand the constant discord. Later I learned about the alcoholism on my mother's side of the family, the mental illness on my father's, as well as the past sexual abuse. This tragic background affected our home life, in spite of the fact that we were Christians.

By the age of two, I knew I was different. I had a congenital eye condition (crossed eyes) and wore glasses. My parents sacrificed to give me good care, yet even with surgery and eye-patch therapy, nothing worked. In the process, I lost the vision in one eye. When my classmates gathered on the sandlot to play games, I was always the last one chosen. I believed I knew the truth: *Something was wrong with me.*

We lived with my grandparents. Grandmom, a godly woman who introduced our family to Christianity, sang to me, and read me Bible stories. Then when I was only

> *You cannot change the past, and you can't always control the present, but you can push the past into its proper perspective and you can face the present realistically.*
>
> (Hugh P. Fellows)

six years old, Grandmom died. Consequently, we moved away from my grandparents' home in the city to the country. Although I felt comfortable at school (I was an honor student), I missed my grandmother, friends, and all that was familiar and fun.

Upon graduation from high school, I enrolled at a Christian college where I met the man of my dreams, Ken Travilla. As Ken completed his seminary work, we were married. Nine months later my father suffered a nervous breakdown. With a broken heart I visited my father, a forty-two-year-old church deacon and respected leader, in a mental institution. I wondered what had happened to our family. *Wasn't it good enough? We followed all the rules. Why didn't it work?*

I was devastated when both my younger sisters left the church and adopted the sixties culture. I tried to be a good wife and mother and help my parents at the same time. My health suffered. To smother the pain, I continued to volunteer at church, assist my husband

with the youth ministry, substitute teach to supplement our income, and entertain as if I were trying to win the Ms. Hospitality Award.

"Carol, how do you do it all?" remarked my friends and associates. These comments spurred me on. It meant someone noticed me and thought I was worthwhile. After nine years serving my home church, Ken took a new position with a larger church in Michigan. We looked pretty good on the outside: mom, dad, son, and daughter. We

> *We need to recognize that all our much-doing is not always fruitful. It is sometimes mindless. Sometimes it is driven. It can be self-protecting. It keeps us going when in fact we should be still—still in order to evaluate and to hear.*
>
> (Charles Ringma, *Dare to Journey with Henri Nouwen*)

longed to do everything right, so Ken and I parented with high control. But often I felt out of control. I just didn't understand. *Why doesn't life work like I want it to? Will I ever measure up?*

Christmas 1971, I was diagnosed with thyroid disease. In my hospital bed on New Year's Eve, I cried, *Why am I here? What now?* For years I had heard others testify about the abundant life in Christ. I wanted it, but didn't know what to do. "Read your Bible and pray," said my spiritual mentors. "Everything will be all right." But everything wasn't all right.

You intended to harm me, but God intended it for good to accomplish what is now being done, the saving of many lives.
(Genesis 50:20)

When I learned that my recovery would take over a year, I was angry with God, my family, and myself. While lying in bed, I reluctantly reached for my Bible. I read the first thirty-six chapters of Genesis and then met Joseph. He had trouble with his family—I had trouble with mine. I reasoned that Joseph knew the same frustration and discouragement I faced. Nothing seemed right. My heart hurt.

In Genesis 50:20 (NASB), I read the words of Joseph to the brothers who mistreated him: "You meant evil against me, but God meant it for good." I reflected on how evil had touched my life. Then I saw my own bitterness and faced my insatiable need to control everything—my parents, sisters, children, and my world.

Lord, forgive me for resenting my life, I prayed. *Forgive me for allowing my anger to become hostility. I know I've trusted my own plans more than I've trusted You. I'm sorry. I don't have much to offer. But if there is anything left that You can use, I give it to You.*

God heard my prayer and I recovered. Then God directed me back to school to work toward a master's degree in counseling. I wanted answers. We were a Christian family, doing all the right things (or so I thought). *Why didn't it work right?*

Use the past as a springboard, not as a sofa.
(Nunn Wiser)

While attending the classes that were necessary for my counseling degree, I grew emotionally. As I grew emotionally, I grew spiritually. I recognized the need for both areas of development. It's not enough to be able to quote Scripture and recite eloquent prayers without an understanding of how the principles of God's Word fit together with how we live.

Every time I relive the deep pain of my past, it always brings me back to my personal need for God's restorative touch. He has stayed true to His Psalm 32:8 promise, and this has allowed me to experience His love and faithfulness in the midst of confusion. Consequently, I can sit with other women, lis-

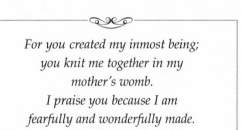

For you created my inmost being; you knit me together in my mother's womb. I praise you because I am fearfully and wonderfully made.
(Psalm 139:13-14)

ten empathetically to their heartache, and then assure them that God cares and renews. God meets each woman right where she is. I believe He uses both the distress and the good to help each woman become who He created her to be.

Several years ago I recognized that the shame of never being good enough had held me hostage. I had always seen myself as a half brick short—never quite attaining what I perceived to be the standard building code of life. Yet I was tired of feeling this way. As I learned more about myself and understood that God had begun working in me years before, I altered my thinking. New thinking led to new feelings. Looking back, I see that the painful experiences contributed to developing me into the woman I am today. Amazingly, as I accept who I am in Christ and my relationship with Him deepens, I no longer feel inadequate or a half brick short.

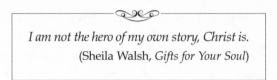

I am not the hero of my own story, Christ is.
(Sheila Walsh, *Gifts for Your Soul*)

There's Power in a Woman's Story

Every woman has a story written with the multicolored pens of her experiences, relationships, perceptions, joys, pain, disappointments, dreams, choices, failures, and successes. Every time we take the time to listen to a woman tell her candid story, we open a door to mutual respect and growth.

There is power in each woman's story, and she maximizes that power when she partners with God. There is power in your story. Your story is unique—distinct from the story of your sister, your mother, your daughter, or your best friend. Likewise, it differs from our stories. No one has a story exactly like yours.

Today I know that memories are the key not to the past, but to the future. I know that the experiences of our lives, when we let God use them, become the mysterious and perfect preparation for the work He will give us to do.
(Corrie ten Boom, *The Hiding Place*)

✎ 1. What parts of our stories or comments do you identify with?

2. What life circumstances prompted you to respond to question one the way you did?

3. Write a short prayer asking God to help you experience the power of your life story.

PART B:
WHERE HAVE I BEEN?

Value in Remembering

In recent years, an old-fashioned tradition has been reestablished: creating and maintaining personal photo/story albums. One album-making organization called Creative Memories focuses on making a "difference in the way people remember, celebrate, and connect."[1] They built a business on the belief that it's important to "preserve the past" in order to help you "enrich the present" and "inspire hope for the future."

God's Word emphasizes the importance of remembering, as well. The word *remember* is mentioned 166 times in the Bible. A common theme throughout the book of Deuteronomy is God's call for His people to remember. God wants you to look back and commemorate your past so that you can learn

> *Teach us to number our days aright,*
> *that we may gain a heart of wisdom.*
> *Satisfy us in the morning with your*
> *unfailing love,*
> *that we may sing for joy and be glad all*
> *our days.*
> *Make us glad for as many days as you have*
> *afflicted us,*
> *for as many years as we have seen trouble.*
> *May your deeds be shown to your servants,*
> *your splendor to their children.*
> *May the favor of the Lord our God rest*
> *upon us;*
> *establish the work of our hands for us—*
> *yes, establish the work of our hands.*
> (Psalm 90:12,14-17)

from what happened and grow. Read the verses from Deuteronomy printed here.

✎ 1. Name five events that God wanted His people to remember.

✎ 2. What do you believe God wants you to remember about your past experiences?

> *"Remember that you were slaves in Egypt and that the LORD your God brought you out of there with a mighty hand and an outstretched arm."*
>
> (Deuteronomy 5:15)

> *But do not be afraid of them; remember well what the LORD your God did to Pharaoh and to all Egypt.*
>
> (Deuteronomy 7:18)

> *Remember how the LORD your God led you all the way in the desert these forty years, to humble you and to test you in order to know what was in your heart, whether or not you would keep his commands.*
>
> (Deuteronomy 8:2)

> *But remember the LORD your God, for it is he who gives you the ability to produce wealth.*
>
> (Deuteronomy. 8:18)

> *Remember the days of old;*
> *consider the generations long past.*
> *Ask your father and he will tell you,*
> *your elders, and they will explain to you.*
>
> (Deuteronomy 32:7)

God encouraged the Israelites to remember their difficult days as slaves in Egypt and how He miraculously rescued them (Deuteronomy 5:15). Each time they faced frightening circumstances, God wanted them to remember how He had previously removed their obstacles to freedom and growth (Deuteronomy 7:18). God told His people to remember their difficult journey through the desert and what they learned about themselves and God during those transition years (Deuteronomy 8:2).

Every good thing that God's people obtain, including material possessions, are gifts from Him, and God asks you to remember this truth (Deuteronomy 8:18). God sanctions looking back at your generational history. He invites you to ask questions and gain understanding about what has shaped your life (Deuteronomy 32:7).

In step two you have the opportunity to celebrate your yesterdays. To accomplish this goal, you need to remember. Yet, you may think acknowledging and talking about the past is a form of complaining or showing disloyalty to parents and ancestors. Perhaps you avoid remembering because it sounds like bragging. Maybe remembering just feels too uncomfortable. Consequently, exercises that cause you to recall your past may seem futile or counterproductive.

However, God says there is value in remembering. To experience the power of your story, it's beneficial for you to look at where you've been during your life, what you've enjoyed, and the memorable and significant events—whether you perceive these as positive or negative. These experiences and situations helped shape you, as did your accomplishments, achievements, and relationships. When you remember and celebrate your yesterdays, learning from past experiences, you have the opportunity to face your future with wisdom and courage.

> *Restoration is not a quick, prefabricated project that is thrown together. It is a deliberate and planned removal of the unwanted, a detailed refining of that which is to be preserved, and an addition of that which was not before.*
>
> (Barbara Stephens, *Psalms for Recovery: Meditations for Strength and Hope*)

Remembering Yesterday

The next exercise can help you become more comfortable with who you are and where you've been so you can honor your past and all that has contributed to making you unique. You will be asked to remember and write down:

- What you enjoyed doing as a child, teen, and adult.
- Your achievements or honors in childhood and adulthood.
- The people who have influenced you through the years.
- The memorable events you experienced as a child and adult.

Although your experiences differ from ours, we are sharing our personal responses, hoping they will help ignite memories for you.

> *Life must be lived forward, but can only be understood when we look back on it.*
>
> (Søren Kierkegaard)

CAROL REMEMBERS

I (Carol) remember a negative experience in my early adult life when a Christian leader betrayed me. However, the ultimate influence she had on me was beneficial because I observed her poor behavior and knew exactly what I did not want to do. It helped me focus on the godly attitudes and actions I did wish to develop. Another person who influenced my life was my older brother's girlfriend. She was kind and accepting during my adolescent years. She had a heart for God and modeled ministry to me. My brother married her, and forty-four years later she influenced me again when she died of cancer—with grace, dignity, and strong faith in God.

As a child, I really enjoyed playing with friends. I still do. Because I was a good student, my teachers encouraged me to skip second grade. I listed this under childhood achievements, and then I realized this might be one of the reasons why I began to feel like I was a half brick short. I always felt out of sync because I was younger than anyone else in my class and graduated from high school when I was only sixteen years old. Other memorable events during my childhood include my grandmother's death, my eye surgery, and needing to wear glasses at the age of two.

JOAN REMEMBERS

During my (Joan's) childhood, my young cousin Jean and I started a greeting-card business while we were in grade school. We walked door to door and asked for orders. Although I was nervous and often left the cold calling to my cousin, I listed this as a childhood achievement. I carried these experiences into my adult life and started several businesses, including a children's store and a design studio. I named these among my adult achievements.

From second grade through college, I took great pleasure in playing the piano; consequently, I listed this in the enjoyment box. Yet for most of the first twenty years of my

> *Our own stories are the composite of all the history, symbols, experiences, and relationships that make our individual biographies: gender, race, year of birth, family of origin, education, vocation, religious faith, marriage, children, socioeconomic status, preferences in music, colors, entertainment, and politics. Some of our stories have very powerful symbols around which almost everything else revolves: physical disability, divorce of parents, winning the lottery, conviction of a crime, being raped, parenting triplets, musical talent, and so on.*
>
> (Leith Anderson, *A Church for the 21st Century*)

marriage, I was without a piano. It left a hole in my life, although I determined that I would be flexible with the situation. Later, when my husband and I purchased a baby grand piano, I was able to enjoy this personal delight again, and I made a tape and a CD.

One memorable event was when I said yes to God at age seven. I remember sitting on the sofa and leafing through the big family Bible looking for answers about how to know God. My parents and Sunday school teachers had taught me about Jesus and the Bible. Then at church one night my dad asked, "Do you want to know Jesus?" Grateful that he had asked, I immediately said yes. Based on my own childhood experience, I believe many children are genuinely thinking about God and want someone to help them develop a relationship with Him. Perhaps it was one reason I wrote a children's devotional book series several years ago.

Both of us feel that our moves have been memorable events for us—often positive and sometimes negative. I (Joan) moved fourteen times during the first ten years of marriage. Carol tells me that she has been transformed by each of their moves—from Pennsylvania to Michigan, then to Minnesota, and from Minnesota to Arizona. Each time they moved across the country, changed churches, and adapted to a new culture, she was required to renegotiate her identity. Consequently, she learned to be gentle with herself while navigating transitions.

Your Turn to Remember

You may be tempted to avoid the accomplishments/honors questions because you think your list of achievements is too short—or too long. We challenge you to embrace your achievements and accomplishments. Although you will want to include your educational and career achievements, think outside the box. What emotional, spiritual, or physical goals have you reached? Perhaps you've been successful at reconciling a relationship, maintaining a long-term marriage, or caring for a terminally ill relative. Consider adding these to your list.

We suggest you ask God to help you remember—to guide your thoughts and responses as you complete these exercises. You may find it beneficial to start writing your responses today and then come back to jot down new ideas as you remember them during the next few days. Allow the memories of significant events to build on one another. This will assist you in recognizing patterns or themes in your life story.

> *People travel to wonder at the height of mountains, at the huge waves of the sea, at the long courses of rivers, at the vast compass of the ocean, at the circular motion of the stars; and they pass by themselves without wondering.*
>
> (St. Augustine)

Recollections of Childhood and Youth

3. During your childhood and youth, what did you enjoy doing?

4. What were the memorable events in your childhood and youth?

5. What achievements or honors did you earn during childhood and youth?

6. Who influenced you during your childhood and youth?

"I am the LORD your God,
who teaches you what is best for you,
who directs you in the way you should go."
(Isaiah 48:17)

RECOLLECTIONS OF ADULTHOOD

7. As an adult, what have you enjoyed doing?

8. What memorable events have you experienced during your adult years?

9. What achievements and/or honors have you acquired during adulthood?

10. Who has influenced you during your adult years?

> *If you call out for insight*
> *and cry aloud for understanding,*
> *and if you look for it as for silver*
> *and search for it as for hidden treasure,*
> *then you will understand the fear of the LORD*
> *and find the knowledge of God.*
> (Proverbs 2:3-5)

IW STORY: DISCOVERING MY CHILDHOOD

What did you enjoy doing as a child? Although a simple question to the other women (I heard the pens scribbling), it was a mile-high wall to me. I simply sat there, unable to remember me as a child. *Just give me a Scripture and a book to study. I can do that.*

The introspection that accompanied this exercise frightened me. I had spent much of my life concentrating on caring for and helping others. I thought this was a noble character quality, and I still do; yet I now realize this behavior was a wonderful hiding place for me. As I focused solely on others, I didn't have time or energy to consider my own needs. My days were spent in an endless endeavor to perfect the roles of my life: wife, mother, daughter, sister, friend. Although many viewed me as having it all together, I lived in an impossible arena surrounded by screaming expectations for myself and others.

With this exercise, I was forced to concentrate on myself. A dim light inside me flickered as I remembered enjoying writing poems, keeping a diary, and reading books as a child. Then I made an enlightening self-discovery: my adult enjoyments of journaling, reading, and desiring to teach and write came from something God had placed inside me from the beginning.

Since I have now given myself permission to discover my once elusive childhood, I continue to learn more about the woman I am right now. It has at times been uncomfortable, yet recognizing the truth gives me immense joy. I am beginning to feel loved and accepted for who I am—not merely for what I do.

DEBBIE HALLOCK, ORGANIZATIONAL CONSULTANT, MOTHER OF TEENAGERS

Part E:
THIS IS WHAT I SEE, LORD.

Learning from Yesterday

Over the years, I (Carol) have noticed that impression without expression leads to depression—or at least intense frustration. Therefore, we want to give you the opportunity to summarize some of the ideas you've gained while completing the exercises about your childhood and adult years. Your yesterdays helped develop your character. They are a part of who you are.

REMEMBERING THE POSITIVE

I (Carol) have been shaped by the influence of a godly grandmother and a resilient mother, early knowledge of Scripture, opportunities to further my education, and a husband who believed in me when I did not. In addition, I think my natural temperament, which values personal spiritual growth, has been a factor in shaping my choices. Ken and I have had the privilege of serving on staffs of outstanding churches in different areas of the United States—this has influenced the way I've lived. Also, I've been shaped by friends who have been like family to me.

1. Skim through the lists you wrote about what you have enjoyed during your life, the memorable events you have experienced, the achievements and honors you have received, and the people who have influenced you. Then complete this sentence: *I have been shaped by the following positive experiences. . .*

REMEMBERING EXPERIENCES PERCEIVED AS NEGATIVE

Often we realize our strengths through our difficulties. Recently I (Carol) talked with a friend I had not seen for several years. She shared how she had been negatively affected by the poor choices of someone else. The circumstances seemed overwhelming and I found few words of comfort. Yet, I was impressed with her coping skills and said, "Pam, you are a strong woman."

She responded, "Yes, I know I am." Although not comfortable to admit, pain is often our catalyst for growth.

2. Again browse through the experiences you listed under the "memorable events" and "people who influenced you" categories in Part B. With a contrasting colored pen or pencil, circle the ones that you perceived had a negative effect on you.

3. Complete the following statement: *The difficulties I have encountered include. . .*

Some of the difficulty I (Carol) have in managing life comes from the fact that I can see through only one eye (due to the childhood problem). Join this with my divergent thinking and it sometimes feels as though I have a learning disability. It's another reason I've felt so different throughout my life. Struggling with these negative experiences made me want to know more about how I learn.

I discovered that there are two kinds of thinkers: divergent and convergent. Convergent thinkers process thoughts logically, in a step-by-step manner. However, the minds of divergent thinkers flit from one topic to another—they often think creatively but have a difficult time pushing an idea through to fruition. Although I have not always appreciated my divergent thinking, it has forced me to focus on developing time-management skills and effective decision-making tools.

Remembering yesterday's negative influences is not meant to set you on a self-pity binge, but to help you accept your uniqueness and learn to celebrate who you have become as a result of your adversities. Indeed, this tool can help you face reality, affirming how God has helped you become a resilient woman.

4. How has God developed your character through the experiences of your yesterdays?

5. Name a time when a lesson you learned from a negative or difficult experience contributed to a ministry opportunity for you.

Moving On

In step two, we shared how God has brought meaning and power to our stories. Then you answered questions and completed exercises that encouraged you to:

- Find the potential power in your life story.
- Reflect on and celebrate your childhood and adult experiences, looking for strengths developed through past opportunities and difficulties.

Before taking the next step, pause to consider where you have been, who you have become, and what God is saying to you now.

Optional: If you feel ready and have the time, write a summary of what you have discovered about yourself to this point.

Step Three: Commit It All to God

PART A:
DO YOU LIKE ME, LORD?

Key Verse:

I praise you because I am fearfully and wonderfully made;
your works are wonderful,
I know that full well.
My frame was not hidden from you
when I was made in the secret place.
When I was woven together in the depths of the earth,
your eyes saw my unformed body.
All the days ordained for me were written in your book
before one of them came to be.
How precious to me are your thoughts, O God!
How vast is the sum of them!

(Psalm 139:14-17)

God and Personal Growth

Do you like me, Lord? I (Joan) wrote in my journal. *You love me, I know, but do You like me? Show me in Your Word where it indicates that You like me.*

Early one morning, a year later, I sat down to study at my desk. Something I read caught my eye: "He rescued me because he delighted in me" (Psalm 18:19).

That's really nice, I thought. I changed the *he* to *I* and the *me* to *you.* "I rescued you, because I delighted in you." *God delights in me?* I looked up the original biblical word for *delight* and discovered that it means "to incline to, to be pleased with, to favor, to like."

I grabbed my journal and penned these words: *Thank you, God. You answered my prayer, the longing of my heart. Something inside me is opening. . . unclenching. . . flying! As a child, I falsely perceived that I was loved out of duty, and not because I was worth liking. I must have transferred this misconception to You. Now I see that You actually want to like me, and this brings a smile to my face—and my heart. Thank you."*[2]

> *He led me to a place of safety; he rescued me because he delights in me.*
>
> (Psalm 18:19, NLT)

According to the key verses (Psalm 139:14-17) for step three, each woman is "fearfully and wonderfully made" by a God who uniquely contemplated and planned her days. It is to this personal, kind, and loving God, who thinks about me with precious thoughts, that I (Joan) commit my life. This truth amazes me because I often have found it easier to recognize God as the good, right, powerful, awesome, and sovereign Creator than to believe that He wants an intimate relationship with me—or that He delights in me.

Perhaps you assent that God loves you, but like me, you have wondered if He likes you—the real you with your unique behavioral traits, passions, and physical features. Yet, according to His Word *and* His gracious acts, the almighty God not only loves you and me completely—He likes us, too.

> *Remember how you were when you didn't know God,. . . never knowing what you were doing, just doing it because everybody else did it? It's different in this life. God wants us to use our intelligence, to seek to understand as well as we can. . . . Each person is given something to do that shows who God is. . . . I want you to think about how all this makes you more significant, not less.*
>
> (1 Corinthians 12:2-14, MSG)

God delights in you with your specific temperament, personality characteristics, gifts, and interests. He wants you to understand who you are, so that:

- you can come boldly and freely into His presence with authenticity and integrity—as the person He designed you to be
- you can appreciate yourself as the recipient of His delight
- the false impressions you have about yourself can be eliminated, releasing you to serve others and take responsibility for your own growth

> *So let us come boldly to the throne of our gracious God. There we will receive his mercy, and we will find grace to help us when we need it.*
>
> (Hebrews 4:16, NLT)

- you can praise and worship Him with your whole being
- you can learn to accept your strengths and your limitations, releasing you from the pressure of unrealistic expectations

With scriptural assurance that God likes the real me (Joan)—with my unique behavioral patterns, personality, thoughts, gifts, interests, passions, and limitations—I have gained permission to ask questions and discover the person God designed me to be. I now realize that it's not ungodly for me to pursue personal growth and development. In fact, I have come to believe that it helps me know God better, which is the longing of my heart.

1. Which statement(s) below best describes your current thoughts about the value of pursuing personal growth? Circle the statement(s) that is closest to your response.

Personal growth interests me and I want to know more.

I already know a lot about this kind of thing.

Personal development programs have helped me in the past.

I think it's self-absorbing to pursue personal development programs.

I believe this would help me in my relationships with God, others, and myself.

IW STORY: DEVELOPING INNER HARMONY

My relationship with God, through His Son Jesus Christ, is what I value most in my life. I have come to believe that my focused times of communication with Him are more precious to Him than all my service for Him ever could be, although good deeds are important.

As I spend time with Him, talking to Him in prayer, listening to Him by reading His Word and being sensitive to His Spirit within me, an interesting thing happens. I then develop a strong sense of inner harmony that leads to personal growth. He helps me understand the truth about myself and my situations and circumstances. He gives me a desire and the permission to read and discover more about how I naturally relate to others and the world around me.

I know that only what is alive can grow—and God has infused me with life. Because of Him, I have the unlimited potential to truly live, rather than just exist and maintain. Knowing Him better has brought lasting positive change in my life and personal growth in the areas that have been most troubling for me such as time management and goal setting, overcoming procrastination, and people pleasing. I value the time I spend with God. I am continually amazed at how He encourages me to develop mentally, emotionally, and physically, as well as spiritually.

KAREN BOOTHE, COMMUNITY MUSIC TEACHER
AND HOMESCHOOLING MOTHER

2. What area(s) of personal growth would you like to pursue? (Here are a few areas that other women have chosen: gaining relationship skills, developing a hobby or interest such as music or craft-making, pursuing time management tools/methods, learning how to journal, developing better nutritional habits, learning ways to exercise.)

PART B:
WHAT AM I DISCOVERING ABOUT GOD'S DESIGN FOR ME?

Different Is OK

Have you ever noticed that people are different? I (Carol) can almost hear your chuckle as you respond, "Of course, it's obvious that people can react differently, even to the same situation." However, I had been married for seventeen years before I fully understood this truth.

My idea of a great evening was to host a party—or at least attend someone else's. My husband Ken's concept of a perfect evening was to retreat to his workshop. I just couldn't understand why he wanted to run away from me. (That's how I saw it, anyway!) As I learned more about the varied temperament and behavioral styles, I began to understand that he wasn't avoiding me. Ken actually *needed* to get away in his workshop or retreat to his garden.

Ken registers as a high introvert on the temperament assessment tests. After working with people all day at his job, Ken regains his energy by spending time alone. Guess what I am? I score high as an extrovert: interacting with people energizes me. Understanding our differences literally changed our marriage. Although we have now been married over forty years, we know we still need to plan and work around this introvert/extrovert reality. Before I say yes to another social engagement, I consider the commitments already on our calendar.

Our respect for one another's needs breathes freedom into our relationship. However, in the last few years I have noticed that the older I get, the more I need alone time—much to Ken's delight! Interestingly, Ken is willing to go out more often. Perhaps this is one of the benefits of mellowing with age.

> *If you know yourself, you can find your God-given place.*
>
> (Jane A.B. Kise, David Stark, Sandra Krebs Hirsh, *LifeKeys: Discovering Who You Are, Why You're Here, What You Do Best*)

UNDERSTANDING BRINGS RELIEF

For years, I (Joan) fought against my tendency to want (and need) to work alone. I knew I really cared about others and wanted to minister to their needs, yet I was not compelled to be with and talk to people all the time. I did all I could do to follow Christ and love my neighbor as myself. I studied Scripture, prayed sincerely, and continued to wrestle with my silent questions. Surely the fact that I enjoy being alone was evidence of my sin-nature, I reasoned.

When my then new friend, Carol Travilla, invited me to take a simple temperament assessment tool and I scored high on the introvert side, I finally understood what was happening inside me. I confided my score to Carol, and initially she expressed surprise. Yet soon she assuaged my lingering doubts with this comment: "Oh, so you have good people skills, then." I felt incredible relief as I realized that I was not unspiritual. I was only an introvert with well-developed social skills. I could not stop smiling.

HOW ARE YOU ENERGIZED? (INTROVERT/EXTROVERT)

You are energized in one of two ways, through extroversion or introversion. You may gain energy by being with other people (extroverts). Or you may be refreshed by being alone (introverts).

1. To help you determine your tendencies, circle the words or phrases in the box below that most describe what you *prefer* to do. Then place an X on the line between the words *extrovert* and *introvert*, at the point where you believe you register on the continuum between the two extremes. Remember that we all can enjoy any of these activities at specific times, but usually not with equal confidence. Choose the phrases that indicate what you usually prefer, especially when you are under stress.

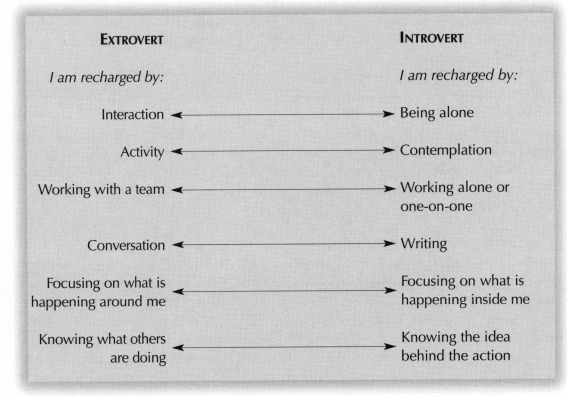

EXTROVERT	**INTROVERT**
I am recharged by:	*I am recharged by:*
Interaction	Being alone
Activity	Contemplation
Working with a team	Working alone or one-on-one
Conversation	Writing
Focusing on what is happening around me	Focusing on what is happening inside me
Knowing what others are doing	Knowing the idea behind the action

2. While marking your X's on the above lines, what did you notice that surprised you or affirmed your behavioral style?

There are no right or wrong temperaments. There are no behavioral styles that are better than others. Everyone has unique ways of thinking, feeling, and acting. Each individual has both strengths and weaknesses. Extroverts do not always need to be with people, but they do usually feel rejuvenated by interacting with others. Introverts do not necessarily long to be isolated on a remote island, yet spending alone time usually rejuvenates them.

OTHER DIFFERENCES

Some folks are intensely aware of their environment and what is happening at the moment. Others tend to look beyond the scenery and their immediate circumstances to concentrate on future ideas and possibilities. Some people react primarily to each day's activities in a spontaneous way, while others prefer to plan and organize. Identifying and understanding your own internal makeup can help you relax and cooperate with God to become the person He created you to be.

> *When we express a willingness to learn, God allows individual circumstances to teach us about our true worth.*
> (Judith Couchman,
> *Designing a Woman's Life*)

There are many different methods for measuring the personal behavior or temperament of individuals. The DISC assessment tool is used by many as a basic assessment

Be Yourself

Are you pleased to be yourself?
Is it an honor and privilege to be
who you are?
I want you to invest in your self-awareness
because you will know Me more fully
when you know and appreciate yourself.

Listen to the song
I placed in your heart when I created you.
Search
and discover the kingdom of God within you.
Talk to your heart,
and be a blessing to yourself.

You will discover the beauty of wholeness,
and your confident spirit will touch others.
I would not have you needy
and crawling on the ground for identity.
Walk tall.

Accept who you are,
and do not attempt to squeeze yourself into
another's image.
You have already been formed in My image,
therefore, be who you are.
It is you I love.

(Psalm 4:4; 139:16-17; Proverbs 16:4; Luke 17:21; John 1:3; 3:16; Colossians 3:10)
(From Marie Chapian,
The Secret Place of Strength
[Minneapolis, Minn.: Bethany House, 1991].
Reprinted with permission.)

tool. Dr. Charles F. Boyd has granted us permission to use the Pace/Priority model (adapted from the DISC method) that he uses in his book, *Different Children, Different Needs.*

Your Personal Style: Pace/Priority Survey

Research indicates that the way we sense, conceptualize, and respond to circumstances can be classified into four basic behavior styles. Social scientists have worked hard to make the questionnaires and surveys credible. When responding to the statements in the Pace/Priority inventory, you may feel that you are contradicting previous answers. Be assured that this is a normal reaction because this is a focused questionnaire.

The assessment tool is based on two major tenets: *pace* and *priority.* *Pace* indicates the way you move through your days—operating in harmony with your internal motor. You may operate at a high speed or move at a slower rate. Although a rush-addicted society seems to value speed highly, in reality a fast-running internal engine is no better than a slower-moving inner motor. They are simply different.

Are You Fast-Paced or Slow-Paced?
If you are a fast-paced person, you are usually comfortable taking risks and making immediate decisions. Your motto may be something like *Let's get going. We've got a lot to do to reach our goal.* You appreciate being in charge. You may have a tendency to overcommit because you enjoy trying to juggle numerous projects at once.

If you are a slower-paced individual, you move at a more deliberate rate because you are careful first to listen, reflect, and then act. Your favorite adage may be *If a job is worth doing, it's worth doing well.* You may dislike unplanned changes and tend to make tentative statements.

Perhaps you're a little confused about this fast pace, slow pace discussion because you feel today's woman cannot help hustling through her roles as employer, employee, executive, friend/neighbor, daughter, church volunteer, community worker, wife, or mother. There never seems to be enough time to get it all done. This pace issue is not merely about how fast you move—it's more about how your internal motor is set. Dr. Charles Boyd writes, "When slow-paced people are forced into fast-paced activities, they often feel emotionally and physically drained at the end of a busy day. Fast-paced people thrive on activity and feel stress when they're forced to slow down."[3]

Because behavior changes in different environments, it will be beneficial for you to have a specific focus while completing the DISC-type surveys in this step. We encourage you to choose a life area and think about how you respond in that setting. For example, you might wish to concentrate on your role at home. Later you can complete this pace survey focusing on another life area such as work or church.

BEHAVIOR PREFERENCES
BASED ON PACE

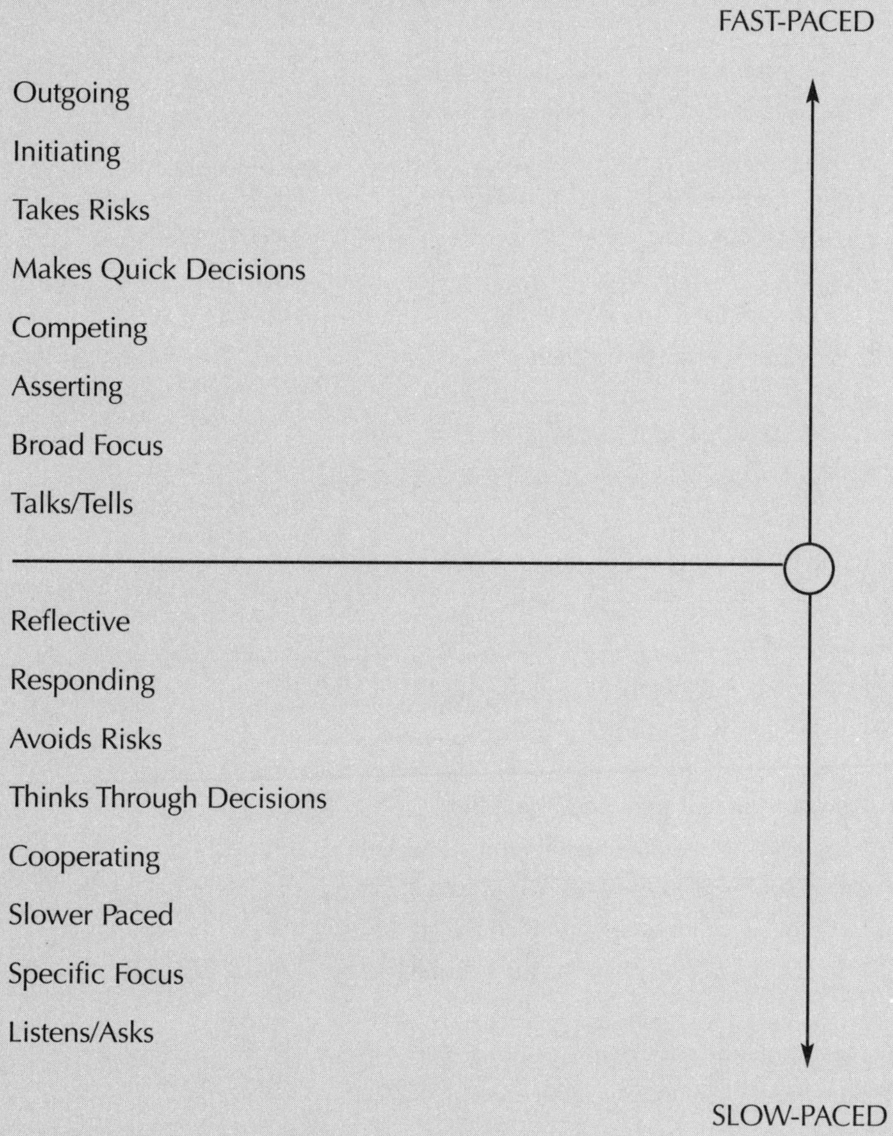

FAST-PACED

Outgoing

Initiating

Takes Risks

Makes Quick Decisions

Competing

Asserting

Broad Focus

Talks/Tells

Reflective

Responding

Avoids Risks

Thinks Through Decisions

Cooperating

Slower Paced

Specific Focus

Listens/Asks

SLOW-PACED

INDIVIDUAL SURVEY: PACE

Identify your focus: (for example, home, work, church, community) _____

✍ 3. To help determine whether you tend to be a fast- or slow-paced person, circle one number in each pair that you feel is most like you.

1. I usually make up my mind quickly. Or. . .
2. I like to take my time in decision-making.

3. I tend to speak quickly and with emphatic statements. Or. . .
4. I tend to speak more slowly and with less-emphatic statements.

5. I find it hard to sit and do nothing. Or. . .
6. I enjoy quiet, do-nothing times.

7. I consider myself to have an active lifestyle. Or. . .
8. I consider myself to have a more low-key lifestyle.

9. I tend to be energized by juggling several balls at once. Or. . .
10. I prefer to do one thing at a time.

11. I easily become impatient with slower people. Or. . .
12. I do not like to be rushed.

13. I am quick to tell someone what I think or feel. Or. . .
14. I am more private about what I think and feel.

15. I like taking chances and trying new and different things. Or. . .
16. I do not like to take chances. I like familiar ways of doing things.

17. I tend to introduce myself at social gatherings. Or. . .
18. I am more likely to wait to be introduced at social gatherings.

19. When others talk, I have difficulty listening. Or. . .
20. When others talk, I listen carefully.

21. I like to be in charge. Or. . .

22. I prefer to follow directions and be supportive.

23. I tend to react more quickly and spontaneously. Or. . .

24. I tend to react more slowly and deliberately.

Record the total number of odd-numbered statements you circled and the total number of even-numbered statements you circled:

_____# Odd/Fast-Paced   _____# Even/Slower-Paced

If you circled more odd-numbered statements, you tend to be more fast-paced. The even-numbered statements describe a slow-paced person.

ARE YOU TASK-ORIENTED OR PEOPLE-ORIENTED?

The second major tenet in this assessment tool is what Dr. Charles Boyd calls *priority*. *Priority* refers to your focus. It represents the motivation behind the activity. *Pace* is the inner engine of your life and *priority* is the inner compass, that which gives direction.

BEHAVIOR PREFERENCES
BASED ON PRIORITY

Independent	Relational
Guarded in Relationships	Relaxed
Reserved	Warm
Likes to Lead	Supporting
TASK-ORIENTED ⟵——————◯——————⟶ PEOPLE-ORIENTED	
Analyzing	Feeling
Time-Conscious	Flexible
Fact-Oriented	Opinion-Oriented
Focused	Easy Going

If you are task-oriented, you concentrate on getting the job done. Often, you make your decision based on the facts and figures about an issue, rather than feelings or opinions. You usually organize your work agenda and stick to your plan, perhaps preferring to work alone. You tend not to talk about other people, unless you're trying to solve a dilemma. Others may perceive you as aloof or cool because you are often more guarded in your personal relationships.

If you are people-oriented, you gain energy by being with others, who in turn may perceive you as relaxed and caring. Often, you are less formal and exacting, so it may not matter to you that the bed isn't made or the meeting doesn't start on time. You may enjoy telling or listening to stories. You notice your feelings easily and are often sensitive about how others act toward you and what they say to you.

Kelli Gotthardt, a business consultant and trainer, contends, " A task-oriented person is concerned that the task gets completed so the people will be taken care of. A people-directed person is concerned that the people get taken care of so they can get to the task." We need both types working together in our churches, homes, schools, and communities.

Learning who and what you are, by God's design, takes the apologies out of life. You become more confident and satisfied with who you are and are not, realizing that God has made you different, even from someone you may admire and wish to be like. It's nice to know who you are so you can deal with yourself.

(Ruth McRoberts Ward,
Self-Esteem: Gift from God)

INDIVIDUAL SURVEY: PRIORITY

Identify your focus: (for example, home, work, church, community) _____

4. To help determine your *priority* focus, circle one number in each pair that you feel is most like you.

1. I approach life in a serious manner. Or . . .
2. I approach life in a playful manner.

3. I tend to keep my feelings to myself. Or. . .
4. I tend to share my feelings with others.

5. I enjoy talking about and listening to facts and dates. Or. . .
6. I enjoy telling and listening to stories about people.

7. I tend to make decisions based on facts, objectives, or evidence. Or. . .
8. I tend to make decisions based on feelings, experiences, or relationships.

9. I tend to be less interested in small talk. Or. . .
10. I tend to be more interested in small talk.

11. I maintain control over whom I get to know and whom I am involved with. Or. . .
12. I am more open to establishing new relationships and getting to know people better.

13. People may perceive me as being a little hard to get to know. Or. . .
14. People tend to perceive me as easy to get to know.

15. I prefer to work independently and alone. Or. . .
16. I prefer to work with and through others.

17. I discuss current issues and the tasks at hand. Or. . .
18. I like to talk about people, stories, and anecdotes.

19. I think of myself as a more formal person. Or. . .
20. I think of myself as a more casual person.

21. Other people view me as a thinker. Or. . .
22. Other people see me as a feeler.

23. I feel best when I am accomplishing something. Or. . .
24. I feel best when I am accepted by others.

Record here the total number of odd-numbered statements you circled and the total number of even-numbered statements you circled:

_____# Odd/Task-Oriented _____# Even/People-Oriented

If you circled more odd-numbered statements, you tend to be more task-oriented. The even-numbered statements describe a people-oriented person.

COMBINING PACE AND PRIORITY

The descriptive statements mentioned in this survey are merely tendencies. These tendencies often vary in intensity or frequency. You (and everyone else) are a combination of behavior tendencies and temperament traits. We don't intend that these questions or tools be used to label you, only that they help you gain knowledge in understanding yourself and others.

These two basic tenets of Pace and Priority can be combined to form four different behavioral styles. When the fast/slow-paced and task/people-oriented diagrams are placed on top of one another, four quadrants are formed, each representing a different behavioral style. This is called the DISC model of understanding human behavior. You can gain an overall assessment of your behavior style by using the scores of your pace and priority exercises.

5. On the chart, mark an X on the arrow representing your higher Pace score. Then mark an X on the arrow indicating your higher Priority score. Next draw a horizontal line through the X on the fast/slow-paced continuum and a vertical line through the X on the task/people-oriented continuum. Make certain that the two lines intersect. By identifying the quadrant where the two lines intersect, you can determine your primary behavior tendency.

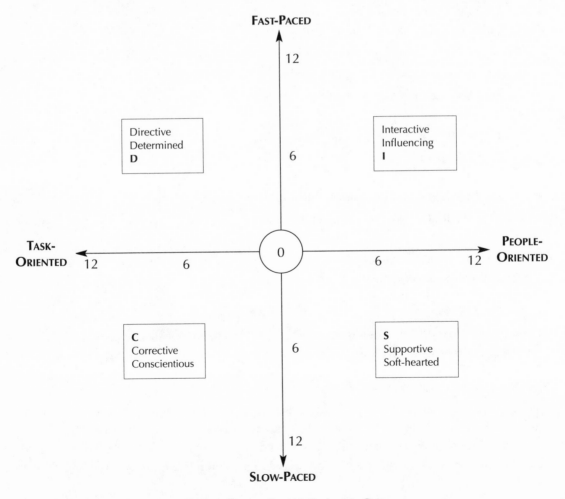

Explaining DISC Differences

See the sample DISC scoring of a woman named Angela. Her pace totals were: Fast = 4 and Slow = 8, so she placed an X on the slow end at approximately the 8 level. Angela's priority totals were: Task-Oriented = 3 and People-Oriented = 9, so she drew an X on the People side at 9. Then she extended a vertical and a horizontal line from those X marks, intersecting in the S quadrant.

Make a careful exploration of who you are and the work you have been given, and then sink yourself into that. Don't be impressed with yourself. Don't compare yourself with others. Each of you must take responsibility for doing the creative best you can with your own life.

(Galatians 6:4, MSG)

Sample: Angela's Preferences—Putting Pace and Priority Together

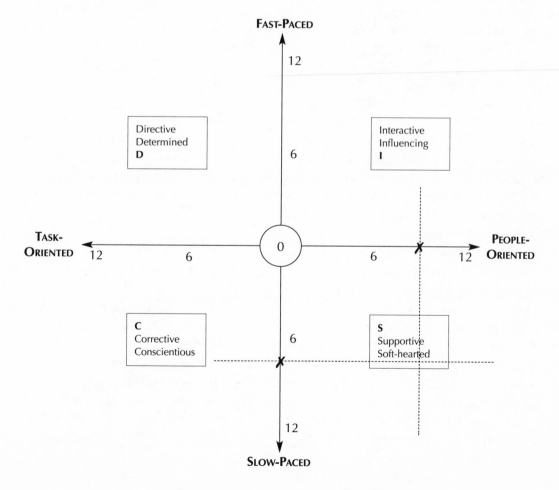

Perhaps you're unsure about how to score your results because you came out balanced (6 and 6) on either the pace or priority arrow. I (Joan) wondered about this because I registered 6 on the fast-paced and 6 on the slow-paced. Dr. Charles Boyd writes, "If you registered 6 and 6 on either survey, it simply means that you express equal amounts of both of these two styles of behavior."[4]

In order to gain more insight about this situation, I asked Cathy Roberts, a professional educator in Colorado Springs, how she counsels the women in this scoring situation. Cathy said, "Over the years, as I have administered the DISC assessment tool with many parents and teachers, I have noticed that when a person is very strong in one area (Pace or Priority), she tends to be equal in the other area. For example, I am definitely a fast-paced person. I am energized by running a three-ring circus and easily bored when forced to manage a one-ring circus. Yet I often feel torn between the task and people-oriented side. When I'm with people, I sometimes think about the tasks I need to finish, but when I'm working on my to-do's, I wish I could be with others."

The courage to be honest is necessary if we're to experience the kind of change our Lord makes possible. Real change requires an inside look.

(Larry Crabb, *Inside Out*)

Cathy's comments helped me understand the dichotomy I often feel inside. I enjoy taking risks and facing new challenges, moving quickly to make decisions and initiate change. However, sometimes I would rather do things one at a time, being careful to listen, reflect, and explore various possibilities before deciding what to do next. If you score equally in one of the two areas (Pace or Priority), look at the descriptions and characteristics on both quadrants. In my case, it would be both the D and the C areas. In Cathy's case it would be both the D and I.

Be gentle with yourself and celebrate the fact that the opposite forces within you can actually temper your behavior. For instance, my desire for immediate, practical solutions to problems is counterbalanced by my genuine need to consider all the options before acting. This dichotomy comes as a natural result of my equal scoring on the pace scale. However, true to Cathy Roberts's observation, I register very strong toward the task-oriented end of the priority scale.

As you complete this effective tool, you are merely getting an overall "read" on your behavior style. You are a unique combination

You were all called to travel on the same road and in the same direction, so stay together, both outwardly and inwardly. You have one Master, one faith, one baptism, one God and Father of all, who rules over all, works through all, and is present in all. Everything you are and think and do is permeated with Oneness. But that doesn't mean you should all look and speak and act the same.

(Ephesians 4:3-7, MSG)

of each style. You behave in different ways in different circumstances. For instance, you who show primarily "D" behavior in a church or work environment may exhibit more "I" behavior at home as a wife and mother because behavior is adaptable. The following DISC chart is an overview of the strengths and challenges of the different behavior styles.

	D	**I**	**S**	**C**
Behavior Emphasis	Directive Determined	Interactive Influencing	Supportive Soft-hearted	Corrective Conscientious
Teamwork Strength	Takes the lead	Networks with people	Provides follow-through	Takes care of the details
Primary Strength	Gets things done; goal-oriented	Motivates and involves others	Effective team player; brings stabilizing force	Analyzes; Accurate and detailed
Communication Strength	Best at initiating conversation	Inspires others; enthusiastic; sometimes one-way	Encourages two-way flow; usually listens	Listens well, especially about tasks
Energized by	Effective outcomes; challenging tasks	Approval; prominence	Appreciation; connection with others	Being correct; accomplishing quality work
Planning Focus	Gets to the point; uses time sensibly	Moves quickly to the next exciting idea	Gets input from others; takes more time	Operates slowly ensuring no mistakes
Behavior When Under Stress	Overbearing and hurried	Disorganized and emotional	Gives in	Retreats; self-critical

You may wish to gain a more in-depth evaluation of how you interact with others. If so, we suggest you complete the longer DISC tool. You may order this tool by contacting Summit Advantage Training & Coaching at the e-mail address: Summit1995@aol.com.

ᏔᎧ 6. On page 71, read through and circle the descriptive words and phrases for fast-paced and slow-paced that are true for you. Do the same for task-oriented and people-oriented on page 73. Then read the chart on page 79, circling the words/phrases under your letter(s) (DISC) that describe you. Finally, write a summary statement about your own pace and priority preferences as you understand them right now.

IW STORY: WHO DID GOD DESIGN ME TO BE?

Because I am a reasonably responsible person with a variety of interests, I often found myself in leadership positions—organizing and directing activities at work, home, and church. I did everything from planning taco dinners for 200 youth to directing the children's musical. Since I had the necessary skills, I felt it would be selfish to say no.

As the years passed, I burned out. Serving was no longer a joy. I would begin a project thinking, *I can't wait until this is over!* I was frustrated and exhausted. The bright spots during that time were teaching a junior high girls' Sunday school class and the times when youth or women came to me with a problem. I loved helping them find answers and encouraging them with God's Word.

Then I took the DISC assessment tool and my scores registered in the "I" box—indicating that I am fast-paced and motivated by influencing others. Details can be especially annoying to someone with this personality. No wonder I was exhausted. I began to understand why it was so rewarding to see those I taught and counseled take steps toward personal growth.

I started saying no to those tasks that clearly fell out of my natural behavior tendencies. Not only were they contributing to my burn out, they were tying up my time and preventing me from doing the things God had equipped me to do. More importantly, I learned that when I took on tasks outside my giftedness, I was denying someone else the opportunity to use their gifts for the glory of God. As I surrendered my life, personality, and gifts to God, I drew into a closer walk with Him—a walk of dependence and joy.

CATHY ROBERTS, PROFESSIONAL EDUCATOR

IW STORY: SLOW-PACED IS OK WITH GOD

I am a slow-paced person who has wanted desperately to fit into a fast-paced world. I do not like being different. Even as a child, I pushed myself to be in step with others. In adulthood I tried to match my perception of what an accomplished woman should be. Success meant doing more, running a little faster, and trying harder.

By the time I was in my late twenties (a young wife and mother), my self-imposed drivenness was forced into slow motion. My life became mysteriously defined by increasing physical pain, depression, sleepless nights, and debilitating fatigue. This picture did not fit my idea of the vivacious, capable woman I believed I needed to be. Doctors found no explanation for my condition.

Then, just before my thirtieth birthday, I read a book filled with testimonies of individuals who had trusted Jesus Christ with personal hardships. I wanted their hope. So with only an eyedropper full of faith, I accepted the forgiveness, love, and leadership of Jesus Christ into my life. My life became one huge prayer. I gained permission to slow down and just *be*.

Twenty years later, I finally received a diagnosis of fibromyalgia and systemic lupus. During those confusing years, I grew to understand how much God valued me apart from what I could accomplish. I empathized with the disabled, elderly, and even young children who could not keep pace with our action-addicted culture. I began to be thankful for what I *could* do rather than envious of what I *could not* do.

Since my diagnosis I have been intentional about getting as healthy as possible. As I live within my specific boundaries, I am steadily improving. Sometimes I say no to meaningful ministry activities in order to say yes to those for which I am better equipped. And now I know the truth: A person with a simple, slow-paced life, like mine, can still be used by God to meet needs in a fast-paced world.

SUE SOUTHERN, BIBLE TEACHER

7. While working through this step, what encouraging insight have you learned about yourself?

8. Is there anything you have become aware of that might be holding you back—keeping you from moving forward with intentionality?

Part E.
I SURRENDER, LORD.

The Turning Point

Gaining information about yourself is useful for many reasons. It can help you choose a career, improve skills, or understand relationships at work and home. However, the ultimate positive outcome of understanding who you are, where you have been, and what you prefer is your surrender to the One who created and liberated you. Surrendering moves you from being self-centered and confined to becoming God-centered and free. You can learn to relax and trust. Until you fully commit yourself to God's ideas and ways, you cannot partner with Him to do what He has planned for you to do. Yet surrendering is a choice. God invites you to join Him in His loving and powerful work here on earth, but He will never force you.

We hope the following stories about intentional women with a heart for God will assist you in gaining the courage to take this vital third step of committing to God all that you have learned and all that concerns you about your life—past, present, and future.

> *God speaks directly to the surrendered heart, building a personal and intimate relationship with the person—revealing His desires, His longing, His plans.*
>
> (Tom Paterson, *Living the Life You Were Meant to Live*)

> *Commit everything you do to the LORD. Trust him, and he will help you.*
>
> (Psalm 37:5, NLT)

Like Abraham

My (Joan's) life changed radically when my husband made the decision to change careers. Although I was disappointed and hurt, I chose to ignore my pain. I thought if I filled my days with activity and accomplishments, I wouldn't have to acknowledge the loss. Yet every time I attended a workshop or seminar, heard a woman teach a Bible lesson, or even contemplated what it would be like to be ministering to others, my heart felt like lead inside my chest.

I tried not to remember my seventh-grade year when I said yes to God's call on my life. Ever since that day when I promised God in my attic bedroom that I would serve Him in full-time ministry, I had worked and planned toward that goal. I dedicated my life to prayer and learning Scripture. I went to Bible college. I married a man who was training for full-time ministry, too. It seemed so right.

Then when everything changed, I couldn't understand. I did not turn my back on God, but I assumed He had changed His mind. As I raced feverishly to pursue other career avenues, I shriveled up inside. Eventually, I realized I could not keep going.

I joined a women's Bible group to study the life of Abraham. One day after class, I headed toward the local car wash. While the huge brushes sloshed against the sides of my car, in my mind I replayed Abraham's story. Then it became clear to me: God was asking me to make a sacrifice, just as He asked Abraham to sacrifice his son. I could have understood if God had asked Abraham to sacrifice something detrimental to his spiritual, physical, or emotional health. But this sacrifice was good, right, and noble. Isaac was God's long-awaited promise—the means by which God would fulfill His great plan for mankind. From Isaac would come the Messiah.

Similarly, I saw my desire to be in full-time ministry with my husband as a good and noble calling. I knew God had called me, yet I sensed God urging me to sacrifice the image of this call on my life. I had envisioned how God would play out His call, and because it wasn't so, I was brokenhearted. That day as I thought about Abraham, I realized that my idea had become more important to me than God's idea. As with Abraham, God desired that He mean more to me than my mission in life— even though what I wanted was not evil.

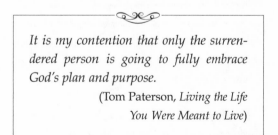

It is my contention that only the surrendered person is going to fully embrace God's plan and purpose.

(Tom Paterson, *Living the Life You Were Meant to Live*)

As I drove through the car wash, I prayed, *OK, Lord. Here it is. I put my image of Your call on my life on the altar.* Unlike He did for Abraham, God did not hold back the knife. My image of the way He would work through me was destroyed that day. God's call on my life was not gone, only my idea of how He should fulfill it. Tears flowed down my cheeks like the water running down the sides of the car.

Suddenly, I felt transformed inside. I experienced release from the overwhelming disappointment and envy I had of others who were doing what I had wanted to do. After that, when I listened to someone teach or speak, my heart felt light. I had sacrificed *my* idea, so I could discover *God's* purpose for me.

> *When one door of happiness closes, another opens; but often we look so long at the closed door that we do not see the one which has opened for us.*
>
> (Helen Keller)

IW STORY: STUBBORNNESS GIVES WAY TO SURRENDER

After twenty-five years of marriage, I faced an unwanted divorce. The pain drove me to my knees, where I discovered unexpected joy in Christ. As a result, I thought I knew—once and for all—the meaning of total surrender to God.

Then two years ago, I started feeling restless—like I might explode. I made the heartwrenching but necessary decision to break up with the man I was dating. After sixteen years of singleness, I was frustrated and angry with God. The loneliness produced an acidic hole in my soul.

In an attempt to heal, I left the church I had attended for over thirty years, resigned from my seven-year position as director with a high-profile company, and gave up a rewarding board position with a nonprofit organization. I rested during the first four months. However, during the next four months, as I searched for a new position, I had to tap into my savings. I was scared. Gradually, I realized I did not have everything under control.

Then as I wrestled with God in prayer one sleepless night, I *got it.* I had my mind made up about what kind of job I needed, and I wasn't leaving the door open to what God wanted. When I acknowledged my self-centeredness, pride, and discontent to God, peace replaced the ulcerating pain I had felt.

Things became clear: I would go back to my church where I had supportive friends. I would go back to my former place of employment—they had graciously assured me I would always have a job there. I was back at work within two weeks. My new position is better than I could have imagined—closer to home and custom-designed to fit my gifts. It is a painful journey from stubbornness to surrender. I have learned that God is incredibly good and I can trust Him with my family, my job, my singleness— everything.

LINDA CHRIST, BUSINESS EXECUTIVE

A New Beginning

Shortly after moving to Arizona in 1994, I (Carol) received two certified envelopes. I tore them open and read both notifications verifying that my Marriage and Family license and my psychologist license were not reciprocal in Arizona. I had spent long days and nights studying for these credentials. Now, I had neither.

Lord, I don't understand, I whispered. *But I know that You give and You take away. You must want to use me in a different way.* I felt the deep loss; still I knew God didn't need my licenses. He wanted my heart—released from what had previously been so important and useful to me. As I stood in my home office and committed it all to God, I had no clue what my next step would be. I was new in town, without my credentials, clinic business, ministries, and familiar surroundings.

Since I had neither the distractions of my job nor any specific appointments, I had extended quiet times with the Lord. Each morning I walked to the park and read the

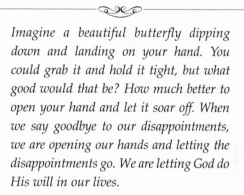

Imagine a beautiful butterfly dipping down and landing on your hand. You could grab it and hold it tight, but what good would that be? How much better to open your hand and let it soar off. When we say goodbye to our disappointments, we are opening our hands and letting the disappointments go. We are letting God do His will in our lives.

(Jan and David Stoop,
Saying Goodbye to Disappointments)

book *Experiencing God.* Although I could not picture my future, I knew God wasn't finished with me and would show me the next steps to take.

That first year, I spent time decorating my home and developing relationships. I decided to become a freelance servant of God. *Just show up,* I felt God telling me. *I'll lead you. You don't need any of your previous labels. I'll be enough.*

I think God speaks during times of transition, disappointment, loss, and change: when you lose your job, or children grow up and leave for college or to start their own families. When marriages crumble or parents age and need extra attention. When spouses die or dreams shatter. When the person who means the most to you rejects your God-given purpose. When you lose a friend. When you're hurt by a spiritual leader. When your doctor says, "It's not good news."

In these times we are faced with a decision: Will we surrender our lives and broken dreams to God? Dare we trust Him? What would it be like if we did? Stephen Arterburn and Dave Stoop, authors of *Seven Keys to Spiritual Renewal,* write, "When we stop trying

Until we give up on our power and agendas and turn our lives and our wills over to Him, we cannot experience or use the power of God to overcome sin in our lives. We must, it seems, surrender.

(Keith Miller, *Hope in the Fast Lane*)

to clean up our shattered hopes, twisted plans, and broken agendas, God has room to work. He can remove the clutter, restore the good, and bring order and beauty out of the chaos. God can be amazingly creative when we get out of His way and give Him room to work."[5]

IW STORY: GROWING THROUGH LOSS

I had tried hard to be a good wife and mother and an active volunteer in church activities. But in our thirty-second year of marriage I sensed my husband distancing himself. I attempted to communicate my confusion and concerns, but his explanations provided little satisfaction for me.

Because I had seen the benefits of professional counseling during my career as a mental health RN, I sought out a Christian therapist. Soon I learned the shocking truth: My husband was having an affair. He chose not to stay in the marriage, and my heart broke.

God, please save my marriage and keep our family intact, I pleaded repeatedly. One day as I was crying out to God yet again, I sensed God's urging: *Jay, give your marriage and all your needs to Me.*

But God, I responded, *You designed marriage for a lifetime and. . .* He seemed to stop me in mid-sentence. *Give it all up to Me—your possessions, your family, your financial security, your marriage, everything.* Something changed inside of me. *OK, Lord,* I prayed. *I see that You actually want me to commit it all to You. So, that's what I'll do. You may have everything.* That was the turning point for me. I got down on my knees and let the tears flow. I asked God to forgive me for doing the leading in our relationship instead of following Him fully and completely.

At the moment of my surrender, I felt a huge weight lift off my shoulders. I experienced peace as I surrendered to Him and allowed His Spirit to lead me.

JAY (JANETTE) MILLS, NURSE
AND MINISTRY VOLUNTEER

FILL MY CUP, LORD

Years ago, after I (Joan) asked God to fill my cup, it seemed instead that He ate my lunch. As I saw my dreams fade away, I worked harder to hold on but eventually lost my grip. I wondered where God was and why He let it happen.

> LORD, you alone are my inheritance,
> my cup of blessing.
> You guard all that is mine.
> (Psalm 16:5, NLT)

Now as I reflect back, I wonder if He could not fill my cup because I already had it full with my personal agenda. I wanted to accomplish great things for God, but I had my own ideas. Perhaps He was waiting for me to empty the unusable contents so He could pour in His plan.

IW STORY: MY COMMITMENT CHOICE

I looked successful on the outside, but inside I was an emotional wreck. I was thirty-nine years old and had lived my entire adult life searching for something that would bring me peace and joy. I read every self-help book that landed on the bookstore shelves. I attended seminars and joined support groups. But I always ended up empty-handed and empty-hearted.

Then I heard about Jesus—several times. At first I resisted. After all, I had tried religion in my childhood and teenage years and it had not worked. Anyway, I was not living the "good little Christian" lifestyle. I wondered if I had ever known God, even though I had gone to church years before.

The message about Jesus that I was getting this time was totally different. It wasn't about how good I was or even if I attended church. This time I heard about unconditional love, mercy, compassion, and how God wanted to have an intimate relationship with me. For the first time, I felt hope—I had the promise of peace. So I made the choice to give Jesus a chance. I turned over my life to Him and we have been best friends ever since.

SUSAN BALDWIN, SINGLE WOMAN
AND BUSINESS OWNER

Responding to God

1. Use the following prayer guide in your alone time with God. Contemplate all that you have learned in the first three steps of this intentional woman process. Talk to God as you finish writing the sentences below. (Try not to be overly concerned with the words you use. Just write down the first thoughts that come to your mind.)

A PRAYER RESPONSE:
I thank You for blessing me with . . .

for giving me the strength to . . .

and the ability to . . .

I can see that I enjoy . . .

I recognize You were there when . . .

I commit my life story to You—past, present, and future. I believe You are a personal God and that You care about . . .

I release to You my tendency to . . .

I admit that I . . .

Help me trust You for . . .

I appreciate Your presence in my life. Thank You for caring, Lord.

Moving On

In step three:
- We both shared one of our turning point stories—and how God desires to have an intimate and loving relationship with us and with you.
- You read the reasons God wants you to understand who you are.
- You completed a self-assessment tool to help you understand your behavioral characteristics and preferences.
- You were given the opportunity to pray and surrender all that you know about yourself—past, present, natural tendencies, and future to God.

Perhaps you're wondering how the above steps can make a difference in the way you face your daily responsibilities. As you work through the exercises in step four, you'll consider the opportunities and roles that compete for your time and energy each day. Before taking the next step, pause to consider where you have been, who you have become, and what God is saying to you now.

Step Four: Consider Your Choices

PART A:
WHAT ARE MY OPPORTUNITIES?

—❧—

Key Verse: "*Come to me. Get away with me and you'll recover your life. I'll show you how to take a real rest. Walk with me and work with me—watch how I do it. Learn the unforced rhythms of grace. I won't lay anything heavy or ill-fitting on you. Keep company with me and you'll learn to live freely and lightly.*" *(Matthew 11:28-30, MSG)*

Age of Overchoice

Today most women face a constant dilemma: too much to do and not enough time to accomplish it all. There are great plans to make, interesting places to go, personal interests to develop, and noble projects to complete. Also, careers to pursue, family problems to address, children to raise, aging parents to care for, financial obligations to fulfill, and ministry work to accomplish. Critical decisions must be made every day about what to do and what not to do.

"I feel pulled in a thousand different directions," lamented a single working mother of three. "I wish God would make twenty-nine hour days. Then I might be able to do it all."

Perhaps you have heard or made similar comments. There never seems to be enough time to do all that you need or want

> *Control isn't really about doing it all. It's about being focused on what you want and pursuing your major goals—not every goal. Control is about making choices and having the courage to let certain things go.*
>
> (Dr. Joyce Brothers)

to do. Yet, you—like everyone else—have all the time there is: twenty-four hours in one day, seven days in one week, twelve months in a year. God will never be persuaded to alter His time plan and give you more hours in the day just so you can accomplish your many goals. Nor will this time-crunch dilemma be solved by simply mastering another effective organizational method in order to stuff more good work into a restricted amount of time.

Several years ago, I (Joan) began to notice that part of my overcommitment problem relates to misconceptions I have about the reality of time. I think I sometimes try to live outside the parameters of time. I do this when I believe that I *should* be able to do everything I dream of doing—for the glory of God and the good of humanity, of course. And then I get myself into a further quandary when I expect that I will do *everything* superbly, every day of my life. When I pause to reflect, I see how unrealistic this is. Actually, I need the boundaries of time and space to help me live in harmony with my humanness.

> *Everything has already been decided. It was known long ago what each person would be. So there's no use arguing with God about your destiny.*
>
> (Ecclesiastes 6:10, NLT)

Carol Van Klompenburg, in her book, *What to Do When You Can't Do It All*, writes, "We need forgiveness for thinking our true self is infinite. We need forgiveness for wanting to be super human. . . . The prayer is not, 'Lord, forgive me for forgetting Cheryl's name today,' but 'Lord, forgive me for thinking I should have total recall.'"[6] You and I do not have total recall, unlimited time and energy reserves, all the right answers, or the abilities and gifts to do everything that needs doing.

> *No matter how well you manage your time, the fact remains: There are still only twenty-four hours in a day. When you try to do thirty hours of work in twenty-four hours of time, the same thing happens to you that happens to an engine that never cools down—you burn out.*
>
> (Holly G. Miller and Dennis E. Hensley, *How to Stop Living for the Applause: Help for Women Who Need to Be Perfect*)

Still, the possibilities and opportunities for today's women increase daily. We live in an age of *overchoice*. We have so many options open to us that it can be overwhelming—and completely unreasonable to think we can do all that looks interesting to us.

Years ago, when our grandmothers were young women, life was usually predetermined. There were exceptions, but most girls knew what to expect: They would get married, have children, become a grandmother, and slow down to get ready to die. Now we live longer and enjoy a multitude of choices about who to be. We are told we can do anything we want to do with our lives—our gifts, interests, talents, skills, education, and experience. So what are all the opportunities that threaten to overwhelm us?

CONSIDER YOUR OPTIONS

~ 1. Start this brainstorming exercise by listing the many different tasks, roles, and jobs that vie for a woman's attention on a daily basis. Think about what *you* do on a consistent basis throughout the year. Consider what your mother, sisters, associates, friends, and neighbors do each day. Think about all eight areas of the Wheel of Life on page 29. Include all the options and opportunities you can think of.

~ 2. Which roles and responsibilities are you attempting to manage at this season of your life? Scan your list and circle ten to fifteen that most describe your life at the current time. You may have one or more significant roles that are not listed here. Add those to the list. In an upcoming exercise, you will be given the opportunity to reduce your roles from the ten to fifteen you circled to a maximum of seven main categories.

> *You don't need to worry about defining the roles in a way that you will live with for the rest of your life—just consider the week and write down the areas you see yourself spending time in during the next seven days.*
>
> (Stephen R. Covey, *The 7 Habits of Highly Effective People*)

CAROL'S CURRENT ROLES

As a result of managing my seven roles, I (Carol) have chosen the one I call Child of God to receive major attention. This role involves my relationship with the Lord. I know I am the only one who can attend to this area of my life. In years past, I tried to live off my husband's spirituality. After all, he had graduated from seminary. Then, through a series of circumstances, God showed me that I need *personal* time in prayer, Bible study, meditation, and worship in order to maintain a growing and intimate relationship with Him.

Another one of my roles is Self-Care Manager. Throughout my life, I have struggled with health issues such as thyroid dysfunction and hormone imbalance. As a result, I have been on medication since I was thirty-five years old. I tend to overdo and suffer the consequences. I know that every piece of food I put into my mouth is a choice I make. I can't blame it on anyone else. I've decided to stay committed to what I need to do to maintain my health, so that I can have the physical stamina to accomplish what He called me to do. I'm the only one who can exercise my body and schedule my time-outs for renewal. I want to care for the body and soul God has given me.

Another role I have is Wife. I include my niche as a pastor's wife in this role. In addition, I count my responsibilities as a homemaker under the category of Wife. I have another role as Mother. In this role, I include my delightful position as grandmother to my four grandsons. Because I have adult children, my mothering role has shifted. I'm no longer a daily managing parent. Consequently, I now enjoy being a supportive friend to my children.

My career as a LifePlan Facilitator and Coach encompasses my Work Life role. I have labeled another one of my roles Friend. This includes my commitment to extended family members and neighbors. I think we sometimes need to combine some of our roles in order to narrow them to seven or less. Still, I believe we need to be realistic and wise about how many different subtitles we can handle. The seventh role I will mention is one I call Writer/Speaker.

My desire is to live as a freelance servant of the Lord in these seven roles. I want to glorify God by being intentional about the decisions I make in each area of my life.

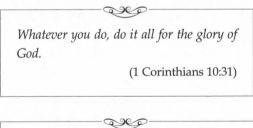

Whatever you do, do it all for the glory of God.

(1 Corinthians 10:31)

JOAN'S ADJUSTED ROLES

Since we first started facilitating The Intentional Woman Workshop, several of my roles have changed. In June 2000 I accepted a full-time ministry position as the International Director of Family to Family, the unique relational sponsorship program of Venture Inter-

To us go the blessings—to God goes the glory.

(Paul F. Keller, *God Grant*)

national, a Christian relief and development agency. I travel regularly to the Middle East and Central Asia, working with field staff and national volunteers. In addition, I travel throughout the States, sharing the story of Family to Family.

This new position meant I needed to readjust my seven roles, so I phased out my role as a ministry volunteer in order to make room for the full-time career position. Also during this time, I became grandmother to a little girl named Annika and a grandson named Max. I added this to my Mother/Mother-in-law category.

Previously, I had listed my music and hobbies under a role I called Woman Responsible for Her Own Growth, but now because I don't have time for these activities, I concentrate on trying to maintain my health under the role I've renamed Self-Care Manager. It is a helpful exercise for me to look at the reality of my seven overloaded roles right now, because, among other things, I recognize that I need to make some intentional adjustments to include music and cultivating friendships (since I have moved to a new location) back into my life. Here's a list showing how my roles changed in 2000-2001.

> *As the pace of change continues to accelerate, "no" may be the magic word. . . . Say no to the extraneous things that distract you from the high-value activities.*
>
> (Odette Pollar)

THEN	NOW
• Resident Rep. for God/Friend of God	Friend of God
• Woman Responsible for Her Own Growth	Self-Care Manager
• Wife	Wife
• Mother/Mother-in-law	Mother/Grandmother
• Friend and Relative	Friend/Daughter/Sister
• Writer/Coach/Speaker — Work Life	International Director/Missionary
• Ministry Volunteer	Writer/Coach/Speaker

Part B:
WHAT ARE MY CURRENT ROLES?

Jesus — Our Ultimate Example

Until you understand the roles you're attempting to manage at this stage of your life, you will continue to find it difficult to be objective about your needs, goals, and realities. It then becomes easy to feel overwhelmed and not know exactly why.

Managing your varied roles will always be a give-and-take situation. On occasion, one role may need more attention than the others. For example: When you have a new baby, your focus will be on your role as mother and you may not be able to give as much time to your career, especially at first. Or perhaps you've experienced a situation similar to one intentional woman whose elderly father suddenly became ill. She needed to concentrate on helping her mother, so her husband and children needed to take more responsibility during that time.

> *Sometimes it helps to know that I just can't do it all. One step at a time is all that's possible—even when those steps are taken on the run.*
>
> (Anne Wilson Schaef, *Meditations for Women Who Do Too Much*)

Sometimes all seven areas of your life will clamor for priority at the same time. You deceive yourself when you expect to always know the right action or the best decision 100 percent of the time. You can reduce your anxiety by adjusting your unrealistic expectations and allowing God to help you flex with your current reality. You cannot be two places at the same time. Neither could Jesus when He lived on earth. He was flexible with His roles—and the daily surprises. Things didn't always go the way Jesus planned; neither do they for us.

1. Read Matthew 14:13-14,23 (printed here). What happened to Jesus' plans to be alone?

> *When Jesus heard what had happened, he withdrew by boat privately to a solitary place. Hearing of this, the crowds followed him on foot from the towns. When Jesus landed and saw a large crowd, he had compassion on them and healed their sick.*
>
> *After he had dismissed them, he went up on a mountainside by himself to pray.*
>
> (Matthew 14:13-14,23)

According to Matthew 14, messengers came to Jesus saying, "We have bad news. Your cousin, John, was beheaded in prison. We just came from the burial."

When Jesus heard these distressing words, He decided to go away by Himself. But the crowds interrupted Him, begging for attention. Jesus remained flexible with His prearranged schedule, attending to the people's immediate needs, healing the sick, and feeding the hungry. When He was finished, He resumed His original plans—to be alone and pray.

Life's interruptions are inevitable. The issue is: How will we react to them? Some surprises are easy to deal with. We can adjust and still meet the scheduled obligations of our various roles. Others are major upsets and totally out of our control. Learning to follow Jesus' example of calm flexibility will help us handle the demands and inevitable interruptions associated with our different roles.

Jesus thought He was going to attend to His role as Self-Care Manager and Son (Child) of God when He planned to withdraw to a solitary place. Yet, when He saw the great needs of the people, He recognized that His role as Healer and Minister war-

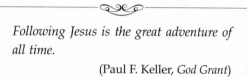

Following Jesus is the great adventure of all time.

(Paul F. Keller, *God Grant*)

ranted immediate attention. He shifted His plans, yet stayed committed to His other roles.

Maybe you need to adjust your life by deleting a role that is no longer important to your current season or adding a new role that has become more significant. Or perhaps you need to back away from a specific role for a brief period because it's keeping you from giving sufficient attention to another area of your life right now.

Roles Pinwheel

Now comes the challenge: reducing your roles to seven (or fewer) from the ten to fifteen tasks, responsibilities, and roles you circled in the list you made at the beginning of step four. Choose five to seven that represent your life roles right now. Making a vertical list sometimes leads to subconscious prioritizing. We don't wish to force you to rank your roles, because they're probably equally important to you. Consequently, we've supplied you with a circular diagram (Roles Pinwheel).

2. In the pinwheel diagram, there are seven adjacent vanes. These vanes all point toward the center of the pinwheel, which represents you. Put your name and today's date in the middle of the pinwheel. In each of the vanes, write one of your seven roles. Having

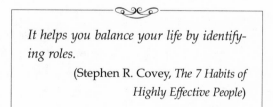

It helps you balance your life by identifying roles.

(Stephen R. Covey, *The 7 Habits of Highly Effective People*)

fewer than seven is normal, depending on your season of life. In this case, you may leave one or two of the pinwheel vanes empty. This will not negatively affect the outcome of the exercise.

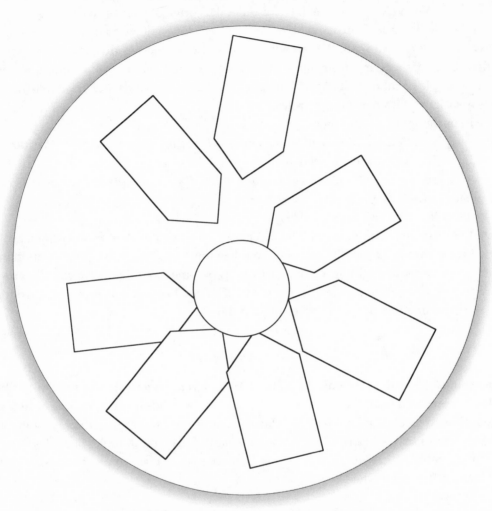

    If you're having difficulty reducing your roles to seven, try this temporary solution: Divide one vane vertically so you can write two coordinating roles in that area. For example, you might want to put your role as wife in the same box with your role as mother. Remember, however, that each time you divide a box you are flirting with overload—too many tasks, responsibilities, and roles. Give yourself time to think about grouping your responsibilities into seven roles. Make it your long-term goal to decrease your roles to seven or fewer. If you're unable to reduce your roles to seven right now, that's fine. If you've reduced your roles to fewer than seven, that's fine too. You'll use this pinwheel again to examine the stressors and supports associated with your roles. We will guide you through the process.

IW STORY: REFLECTION AND ROLES ADJUSTMENT

I have often described myself as being *reflectively challenged*. Consequently when I went through a dark spell in my life, the last thing I wanted to do was *reflect* on it. I had just lost my mother to a nine-month struggle with cancer and spent Christmas Eve in the operating room—as a patient rather than my usual role as doctor. Because processing loss does not come easy for me, I threw myself back into my comfortable routine of working long, hard hours and overextending my commitments.

Call it a mid-life crisis or burnout—either way the result was the same. At age fifty-one, I realized I was totally out of balance and needed help. Pausing to clarify my passions, goals, and roles was just the treatment I needed, so with the help of friends, I reflected on how God made me. I love to learn and strategize. After I allowed myself to acknowledge my passion for studying and teaching the Word of God, I gave more time to this role. I also realized that I could apply what I taught from Scripture to my role as a family physician and vice dean for the medical school.

As a result of what I gained from my guided reflection time, I entered a master's program in bioethics. Studying current bioethical issues such as physician-assisted suicide and cloning has reenergized my life. Serving on the board of Phoenix Seminary, I have been able to use my organizational and strategizing skills.

I learned that God really can use a reflectively challenged person for His kingdom work. I adjusted my varied roles so I could begin to experience healthy balance in my life. In the process, I discovered that sometimes reflection time is worth the trouble. For me it means pausing to ask necessary questions and then listening to the truth—from within myself, from my friends, and from God's Word.

JACQUELINE CHADWICK, MD
VICE DEAN, UNIVERSITY OF ARIZONA,
COLLEGE OF MEDICINE,
PHOENIX CAMPUS

BENEFITING FROM YOUR ROLES PINWHEEL

I (Carol) find great benefit in looking at my seven roles each week. It provides me with guidelines for decision-making and helps me recognize which area demands priority attention at any given time. When I contemplate my roles, I gain insight about why I'm confused (or pleased) in a specific area of my life.

In addition, my roles have become the basis for my prayer life. I talk with God using my roles as a prayer list: Mother, Friend/Neighbor, Wife, Self-Care Manager, Child of God, Coach/Writer/Speaker, LifePlan Facilitator. As I pray about the day before me, the Lord brings to my memory a call I need to make, a letter or check I need to write, or an appointment I need to schedule.

In Matthew 11:28, Christ invites us to come to Him and find renewal, working with Him to learn how to live gracefully. He promises not to overburden us but to allow us the freedom and space we need to develop without fear. I know that by watching Him, I will continue to learn insight about how to balance my roles.

IW STORY: LEARNING TO LIVE WITH MY ROLES

I felt disorganized. As a stay-at-home mother of two young sons, the wife of a traveling executive, and the part-time caregiver for my elderly grandmother, I was busy all the time. In addition, our family had just moved to a larger home, and I was coordinating the extensive remodeling efforts. Still, I was not sure that what I was doing each day had lasting value. Then I did the Roles Pinwheel exercise.

I identified my seven current roles: wife, mother, child of God, personal caretaker, home decorator, friend/neighbor, member of a large extended family. Then I realized that these roles were exactly what I wanted to be doing. What an affirmation to know that I am living out my values and making daily choices that support who and what I want to be.

Before I felt like I was wasting time. Now the tasks that used to frustrate me, like waiting in the doctor's office, take on new significance as I accept my God-given roles at this season of my life.

JILL TRAVILLA, WIFE AND MOTHER

STRESS VS. SUPPORTS

For years I (Joan) pursued activities and work situations that really did not fit with my personal values or aspirations. In order to change this self-defeating reality, I took frightening yet intentional steps. I asked God to give me courage and to show me things about myself that were holding me back. He granted me the boldness I needed to move into new career areas and expanded my world by giving me ministry work with projects in the Middle East and Central Asia.

Recently, when I completed my own Roles Pinwheel exercise, I was amazed and grateful at how different my life has become. I am now living many of my dreams. Yet my stress level is high. I wondered: *Should I relent to the pressure and turn my back on the work God has given me to do?* Then as I completed the Stress vs. Supports part of the Roles Pinwheel tool, I saw the problem: I have very few supports to balance out my stressors. The solution: Take intentional steps to get the supports I need in order to manage the new tasks God has given me.

Below is a list of activities that other intentional women have used as supports (personal coping resources) to counteract everyday stress.

Laugh	Sing in the choir	Take classes	Help a neighbor
E-mail a friend	Join a support group	Exercise	Listen to tapes
Decorate a room	Pray	Garden	Study the Bible
Cook for fun	Spend time alone	Journal	Participate in a sport
Read a book	Lose weight	Volunteer	Daydream
Go shopping	Organize photos	Play golf	Relax with friends
See a counselor or a life coach	Take a car ride	Play the piano	Entertain

3. Circle the activities that you have used as stress relievers in the past. Remember, an activity may be enjoyable for one woman, yet stressful for another.

YOUR TURN AGAIN

👈 4. Turn back to your completed Roles Pinwheel.

- Use a regular pen or pencil for the first part of this exercise. On the end of each vane, draw lines attached to circles that represent persons and activities involved with that role. For example:

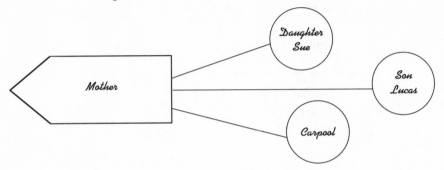

- Repeat this process for each role.

- Most relationships and life activities include stressors and supports. Reflect on each person and activity you have identified. With a red marker or pencil, color in the portion of the circle that represents the amount of stress you experience in that relationship or activity.

- Use a blue marker or pencil to color in the portion of the circle that represents the amount of support you experience in that relationship or activity.

For example:

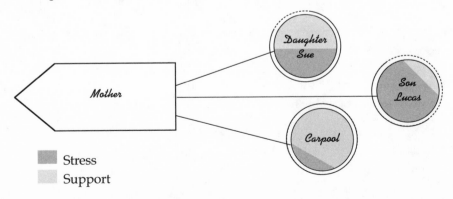

Your Roles Pinwheel may now look something like this:

Roles Pinwheel: Stresses vs. Supports

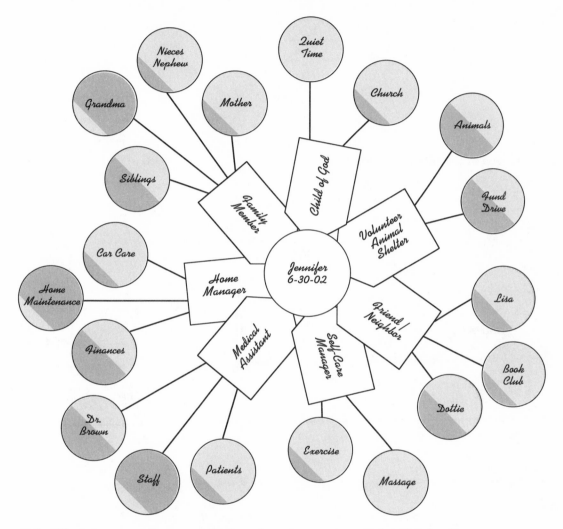

🖎 5. What do you notice as you look at the colors on your Roles Pinwheel?

6. Can you identify a thread of common stressors—or is the stress different for specific roles? Consider stressors that affect you physically, emotionally, mentally, or spiritually. List a few here.

7. What are some ways you receive support? List the people, places, or activities that you experience as supportive.

8. Are there one or two specific changes you might make to reduce your stress level and/or increase your support? Jot them down.

This exercise can be used whenever you begin to feel overwhelmed or confused to help you gain a clearer picture of the balance between your stress points and supports. It can help guide you in determining what roles need attention and what steps you may need to take next.

> *The greater the amount of stress you feel, the more you need to use all your coping resources. The more effective your coping resources [supports], the greater your satisfaction.*
>
> (Carlson Learning Company,
> *Coping & Stress Profile*)

!W STORY: FREEDOM TO CHOOSE

The Roles Pinwheel exercise was a rude awakening for me—when I saw on paper all the ministry activities I was involved in. Twelve responsibilities came to mind without any effort at all. This, on top of being the mother of three small children, a pastor's wife, and a part-time business consultant.

The other thing I noticed was how intertwined my ministry was with my relationship to my husband, Richard. I felt instant agitation. Though I wasn't sure why I was agitated, my feelings grew as the days wore on. Finally, I realized that I felt grossly underappreciated for all the work I did to enhance my husband's ministry.

In my efforts to communicate this to Richard, I saw how terribly codependent I was. (He helped me get there.) I was trying to fix it all so he would be less stressed and enjoy the ministry more. It felt like I was regressing to the early days of our marriage when I believed I was a better-equipped leader than he was. We had worked hard on learning and accepting our individual strengths. Yet for some reason, the old feelings had subtly crept back during a time of crisis.

After acknowledging what I saw about my roles, stresses, and supports, I began to feel better. I don't feel as responsible (in the unhealthy, people-pleasing way) for the ministry. I feel freedom to make choices about how and where I am involved. I don't have to do something merely because I have the ability.

KELLI GOTTHARDT, TRAINING CONSULTANT

The LORD was my support.
He brought me out into a spacious place.
(Psalm 18:18-19)

PART E:
I WANT TO MAKE WISE CHOICES, LORD.

Putting It All Together

The key objective of step four: Consider Your Choices is to help you connect what you've learned so far from this workbook. You have paused to consider:

- Where you are right now—step one
- Where you have been and what has shaped your life—step two

- Who God designed you to be and how He wants you to trust Him—step three
- Your opportunities and roles at this phase of your life—step four

Your season of life, behavior preferences, life experiences, passions, and perceived calling from God work together to help you make intentional decisions about your future.

YOUR CURRENT SEASON

"You have been shaped and fashioned for a specific mission, but this mission changes from season to season in your life. Your giftedness does not change, but its *application* has phases. These phases are as much a part of God's creative process in you as any other aspect of your being," writes Tom Paterson in his book, *Living the Life You Were Meant to Live.*[7] Recognizing and accepting your current phase of life empowers you to be more realistic about what you can accomplish.

1. Write down several phrases that describe your current season. (For example, empty-nester, newly married, widow, new mother, grandmother, single, college student.)

YOUR REALITIES AND PRACTICALITIES

You need to consider your unique realities and practicalities in order to make wise decisions about your future. The following are the realities and practicalities of several women in one of our recent IW workshops:

- One woman has two preschoolers and is pregnant with her third.
- Another is undergoing chemotherapy for cancer.
- Another lives in Arizona during the winter and Minnesota during the summer.
- One woman has a husband who is not a believer in Jesus Christ.
- Another just lost her job of ten years.
- Another is married to a professional football player.
- Another needed to go back to work full-time since her husband's job was downsized.
- One woman has three children in college at the same time.

2. Write down three to five realities and practicalities about your current life situation. (Perhaps you would like to use the above examples to get you started.)

YOUR PASSIONS

Your passions bring vitality and zest to your life—they energize you.

3. Write five exciting activities that would cause you to jump out of bed in the morning if you knew these events were on your schedule for the day. This list will give you an overall idea about your passions.

> *It isn't the size of your passion that counts, but whether or not it is from God. The world can use all kinds of help.*
>
> (Jane Kise, David Stark, and Sandra Hirsh, *LifeKeys*)

IW STORY: PUTTING IT ALL TOGETHER FOR ME

After I completed the "Putting It All Together" exercise, a lightbulb blinked on in my mind. For the first time I actually connected my current realities with my goals and intentions—and how my daily activities fit with my big picture.

Of course, I knew I was a busy mom of a two-year-old and a one-year-old, with another one on the way. In addition, I acknowledged that all my extended family lived back east and I missed their love and support. However, I had never made the connection between these facts and my dreams and desires. I was in the habit of just brushing these little daily life circumstances away as not big enough (on their own) to affect my overall life goals.

Then when I looked at the uniqueness of my season and my realities and practicalities, I realized that my current situation was neither good nor bad—it just was. My realities automatically affect the way I plan, set goals, and reach my objectives. For example, one of my goals was to get back into a workout routine. Yet, reality dictated that I needed to take care of my children.

I wanted to spend more time with my husband and kids.

Consequently, I began to think about ways I could be intentional about becoming active *with* my family. What a difference this new way of thinking made. No longer did I feel like fighting my circumstances. Now I can embrace my current season with the full assurance that this phase will not last forever. I feel free!

HILLARY NELSON,
PASTOR'S WIFE AND MOTHER

Yes, You Do Have Choices

POWER TO CHOOSE

For years I (Joan) believed I didn't have much choice about who I should be or what I should do. I had the impression that to be a good Christian wife, I must go along with whatever happened around me and to me. Consequently, I didn't think I had the right to make deliberate decisions about what I wanted to do or what I wanted to become. This misconstrued philosophy worked for me at first. But over the years my suppressed frustration and anger—at not being able to be the person I thought God wanted me to be—resulted in total burnout.

I begged God for help, and over the next few years He assured me that I *do* have choices. I learned that He *expects* me to take responsibility for my own development and that means I need to take steps to make decisions that no one else can make for me.

I know I'm not the only woman who has had difficulty believing she has choices. When I talk to women one-on-one, I hear similar stories. When I assert that everything we do is a choice, I often meet resistance. "No," said one friend, "I do not have the choice to walk away from my difficult marriage."

Sometimes it takes several months for the truth to sink in (as it did with my friend). However, many women finally understand: Indeed they could choose to walk away— although they may not. It is within their personal power to make a decision to stay and make the best of their current situation. It is also within their power to leave and face the consequences.

>
>
> *I was forced to face reality. Because of my unmet expectations, I had been postponing any action. Because I didn't like what I saw, I was failing to do anything to try to improve the situation. I wasn't dealing with the circumstances, and I wasn't prepared to because this was not the way it was supposed to be. As long as I had that attitude—as long as I didn't accept reality—no progress for solution was possible. As long as I wished for reality to be different, I failed to handle the problem.*
>
> (Elizabeth George,
> *Loving God with All Your Mind*)

MAKING INTENTIONAL CHOICES

There are at least three ways to respond to life's circumstances. One response style is to remain passive: Just let life happen. Another response is to question what is happening. A third response is to do something about what is happening. I (Carol) believe that many women respond in the first way (just letting life happen) until this doesn't work well for them any longer.

Then they begin to question and consequently come face-to-face with problems they haven't noticed before. At that point, women have a choice (and by the way, so do men). Some women (including myself, in the past) choose to become a victim of their circumstances. Usually when we choose this option, we do any or all of the following: whine, complain, blame, give up, deny, and stay miserable. Indeed, we have a choice about how we'll respond. In the ten years I worked in private practice, I saw many women who could not get beyond this point.

I met other women who, after realizing they had choices, moved ahead to become intentional. An intentional woman notices, feels the discomfort, questions, considers her choices, clarifies her options, gets support, and takes the next step forward.

JOAN'S EXPERIENCE

I remember when I (Carol) facilitated a LifePlan for Joan several years ago. The LifePlan is a two-day, intensive, one-on-one time spent looking at where you are now, where you have been, where you are going, and where you would like to be. (Yes, this IW workbook is a group process similar to the LifePlan.) The first day of the LifePlan (LP) includes several mentally and emotionally exhausting exercises. As we came to the end of the first day, Joan said, "I feel obstinate." My immediate response was, "Yes, I know; I was just about to tell you we're through. This isn't working." I chuckled as I said this, but it really wasn't funny.

Joan had built a wall of defense to protect herself. After we discussed it, we decided we could not continue through the entire LP process until Joan made some intentional decisions about her health. Even though she was passionate about serving God and wanted to move forward, she and I both knew that she needed to address her newly diagnosed fibromyalgia and perimenopausal problems before she made any purposeful career or ministry decisions.

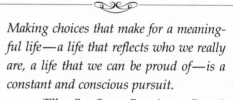

Making choices that make for a meaningful life—a life that reflects who we really are, a life that we can be proud of—is a constant and conscious pursuit.

(Ellen Sue Stern, *Running on Empty*)

We talked about options, we drew up a simple plan for her role as Self-Care Manager, and she flew back to Minnesota from Arizona. (This was before she moved to Arizona.) When she arrived home, she implemented the plan: She had to admit her need, let other people know, do research about medical plans and options, and readjust her schedule. The plan demanded commitment and follow-through. She agreed to a special health program at the Sister Kinney Clinic in Minneapolis, where she had appointments two to three times a week for six weeks. She found ways to balance the medications, learned methods for managing the symptoms, and began a water exercise program. In three months, we got together again and finished making next-step plans for the other areas of her life.

Just like Joan, you live with the power of choice. Some of your decisions may be difficult to make, yet it's an awesome privilege to activate this God-given power. You need not move through the hard steps alone, for Christ promises to teach you how to live "freely and lightly."

IW STORY: I HAVE CHOICES

During the past ten years, my husband has had seventeen surgeries, including heart, cancer, and brain. I came to accept the challenges of those difficulties and forgot that I still have choices in my life, even in and around the demands of the circumstances. I have said yes to returning to a proactive stance instead of living totally in a reactive mode. I found that even with great needs at home, I can fit in a part-time job working with a Christian ministry. That step has opened up opportunities to be involved in a women's group, and now I lead a Bible study for couples in our home. My life felt like it was on hold for a while, but now I recognize that there is room in my life to move ahead with God's personally designed plans for me.

BONNIE OLSEN, ADMINISTRATIVE ASSISTANT

4. Complete this sentence by writing your name in the blank:

I, _____, do have choices.

5. If you want this to be a permanent personal philosophy that changes the way you make decisions, but you find it difficult, try this simple idea. Print the above statement on several sticky notes. Then place them in areas where you will see them often. You may want to attach a note to your computer, near your telephone, on your dashboard, bathroom mirror, journal or day-timer, refrigerator, washing machine, or nightstand. Where will you put your notes?

IW STORY: CHOOSING TO CHANGE

Newly married and employed in full-time ministry with my husband, I felt happy and excited that I was using my gifts. I loved the opportunities I had to speak, counsel, plan events, and nurture young Christians. My husband and I shared the household chores and I was content with my daily life.

Then after our first child arrived, things changed. As delighted as I was to have a darling baby girl, I was less than thrilled to be suddenly stuck home all day with no adult companionship and now in charge of all the routine housework. As a creative extrovert, I hated the loneliness and monotony.

Because getting household help was not an option, I felt trapped. Consequently, I spent some time complaining to the Lord about my predicament. Then I had an *aha!* Maybe I could try looking at domesticity as a spiritual discipline. I determined to do the mundane things as a "sacrifice of praise" and let God transform my attitude.

Soon I recognized that God was developing a new sense of patience and self-discipline in me. I had made a conscious choice to change the way I faced my circumstances and I no longer felt so frustrated. Little did I know thirty years ago that I would exercise this same discipline repeatedly throughout my life—as a young widow supporting myself and two children, as the CEO of the company my husband left behind, and most recently in my new marriage with the challenge of a blended family.

HELEN SIMS STEINKAMP, DIRECTOR OF
MARKETPLACE WOMEN

> *Through Jesus, therefore, let us continually offer to God a sacrifice of praise—the fruit of lips that confess his name.*
> (Hebrews 13:15)

Moving On

In step four:

- You listed the various tasks, opportunities, options, and roles that vie for a woman's attention on a daily basis.
- You narrowed your roles at this season of your life to seven or fewer.
- You determined your supports and stressors.
- You listed your realities, practicalities, and passions.

God has given you the privilege of deciding for yourself. The joy of positive change will be yours to claim.

PART A:
WHAT WILL IT TAKE TO GROW?

❧

Key Verse: I pray that your hearts will be flooded with light so that you can understand the wonderful future he has promised to those he called. (Ephesians 1:18, NLT)

Growth Is Rewarding

Life is always changing. Yet you can choose your response to what happens in and around you. Growth in your personal life *and* in your relationship with God begins with a desire. In step five, you will contemplate what you desire. Once you identify your aspirations, you will then need to determine what discipline (or plan of action) will help you accomplish what you want to do. Once the new habit, relationship, or skill becomes an integral part of your everyday life, you'll experience the rewarding aspects of growth.

I (Carol) remember the day I looked at my Wheel of Life and noticed that the "fun and recreation" area registered low. My husband and I had always been a driven ministry couple. We devalued taking time for recreation because we were taught that "you should not play until your work is done." In many career pursuits, work is rarely completed, but in ministry it is *never* completed.

I can't play golf with my husband because of my limited eyesight, so I asked myself what I had enjoyed doing as a child. Without hesitation I thought about how I had loved to ride my bike. I mentioned to Ken that I would like to begin riding my bike again. Because we were both experiencing symptoms of the empty nest syndrome, he recognized the need for us to have a shared "fun" interest. Today the fun and recreation section of my wheel (which correlates with my Self-Care Manager role) registers a 9 because of the intentional steps I took to increase my satisfaction in that area. Ken and I just returned from our first bike tour in Napa Valley. This enjoyable experience resulted from that first intentional step I took fourteen years ago.

As it has for me, growth and life satisfaction can occur for you when you identify a need, develop a strategy to meet the need, and then delight in the outcome. Growth *is* rewarding. But it doesn't happen overnight. It is a process.

GROWTH IS A PROCESS

"Why is everything always a process?" asked Pamela. "Isn't anything ever *done*? I just want to forget what was and move forward. I don't *do* process very well."

Like Pamela, I (Joan) have had a difficult time accepting the fact that lasting change is a process. I want instant healing, instant excellence, even instant maturity. At times avoiding struggle has seemed more valid than pursuing genuine growth. I have wished I could just wake up in the morning and it would all be over.

Processing life—with the good, painful, and disappointing—is an annoyingly slow procedure sometimes. Although the process is always worthwhile, sometimes it takes me to frightening places where I feel unfamiliar emotions and think uncomfortable thoughts. It takes courage to move beyond conditioned attitudes and behavior.

You and I are surrounded by society's message to hurry up and live. Combine this with the inner pull to avoid pain, and we may begin to believe the false philosophy that faster is always better and that hardship is to be avoided at all costs.

> *Growth is an erratic forward movement. . . . You are capable of great things on Tuesday, but on Wednesday you may slide backward. This is normal. Growth occurs in spurts. You will lie dormant sometimes. Do not be discouraged. Think of it as resting.*
>
> (Julia Cameron, *The Artist's Way*)

> *It is slow work. . . . The only way we can be of use to God is to let Him take us through the crooks and crannies of our own characters. . . . How many of us have learned to look in with courage?*
>
> (Oswald Chambers, *My Utmost for His Highest*)

GOD SANCTIONS PROCESS

If God had sent His Son to accomplish His redemptive work during a weekend retreat, perhaps Jesus could have escaped much of the discomfort. Instead God chose for Jesus to arrive as a baby, become a teenager, and confront young adulthood. The faultless Son of God left perfection with His Father to face earth's reality: sickness, death, abuse, and unbelief.

During Jesus' thirty-three year journey here on earth He experienced limitations and discomfort, as we do. You and I have time and space restrictions. So did Jesus. You and I need food, sleep, rest, and caring relationships with other people. So did Jesus. I know that to nourish my soul and understand God's will for my life, I need time spent praying and listening to God. So did Jesus.

The road to the cross was long and difficult at times. Likewise, the intentional woman's journey to lasting positive change can be tiresome and perplexing. When I (Joan) realized that God sanctions process, I began to relax and accept that progress takes time and involves detours. Sometimes I take substantial steps forward and then something triggers the old response strategies and I fall back. But Carol reminds me that usually the regression is not all the way back to where I started. I always have the option to pick myself up right where I am and begin again.

As I become intentional about combining what I have learned about myself with the truth about who God is, my action steps actually glorify Him. And in the process, I enjoy God and life. This is what energizes me. At the same time, this is what calms me.

1. Review the prayer you wrote in response to the Bible verse you chose during step one on page 41. What has God been showing you since you prayed this prayer?

> *But Jesus often withdrew to lonely places and prayed.*
>
> (Luke 5:16)

> *I ask—ask the God of our Master, Jesus Christ, the God of glory—to make you intelligent and discerning in knowing him personally, your eyes focused and clear, so that you can see exactly what it is he is calling you to do.*
>
> (Ephesians 1:17, MSG)

> *Any relationship, to remain alive, requires at least two living participants. In this case, a God who does not exist as a convenience, magically giving us what we want, or feel we deserve, but a God who simply is—the ground of being, the great "I AM." And with this God...we can come into our own, no longer in fear of "being nothing," but people who can listen, who can change, who can be surprised.*
>
> (Kathleen Norris, *Amazing Grace: A Vocabulary of Faith*)

IW STORY: GOD'S MURAL OF MY LIFE

This five-step discovery process is like viewing the Great Master's painting of me and my life. It is as though I stand before a huge mural entitled Susan Rogers. As I respond truthfully to each question and complete each exercise, the light broadens to include another section of the canvas. I have begun to understand what God has been doing all these years.

It confirms *and* illustrates my life verse: "'For I know the plans I have for you,' declares the LORD, 'plans to prosper you and not to harm you, plans to give you hope and a future'" (Jeremiah 29:11). Now I look forward to the future with renewed hope and courage. I trust that the Master Artist will complete my life mural for His glory. I find joy in knowing that with each new intentional action I take, I am cooperating with God in what He yet desires to do in my life.

SUSAN ROGERS, BIBLE STUDY LEADER

2. After looking over your Roles Pinwheel exercise in step four, list your current roles in the first column on the following chart. In the second column describe your present reality in that role. Then identify a need or desire related to that role and jot it down in the third column. It's possible that you don't sense a need for change. In that case, you might write, "I want to continue what I am doing."

There are no right or wrong responses. You need not write everything related to a specific role. Try to write the first thing that comes to your mind. You can do this exercise again later—tomorrow, next week, or in ten years. Perhaps you will wish to concentrate on only one or two roles right now instead of five or seven.

A Master Artist, God will weave together all our joy, sadness, and experience to create a portrait of our life with depth, beauty, sensitivity, color, humor, and feeling.

(Melody Beattie,
The Language of Letting Go)

*Where does understanding dwell?
God understands the way to it
and he alone knows where it dwells.*
(Job 28:20,23)

Lord, all insight originates with You. You are the source of understanding, good judgment, and wisdom. Please turn on the light for me.

Current Role	Present Reality	Need for Change?

3. From the chart, choose one need that you would like to address. (To help you decide, consider any recurring concern, worry, or thought you have encountered during this study.) What do you want to do to help meet this need?

> *We need to discipline the desire in order to experience the delight.*
>
> (Carol Travilla)

> *That is how I view our spiritual journey, just taking the next step. I find that hard. I want to know the whole game plan. I want to know what roads I will be on, where they will take me, and how long it will take, and when it will happen. But as a follower of Christ, all I am called to do is to take the next step.*
>
> (Sheila Walsh, *Gifts for Your Soul*)

Obstacles to Intentional Living

"When we have a heart for God, whatever thwarts us can become what teaches us to know and love God," writes Jan Johnson in her book, *Living a Purpose-Full Life*. Johnson explains, "When I teach at retreats, women say to me (too often), 'This sounds terrible, but I'm glad you've been through so much so you can share it with us.'"[8] Your struggles (after propelling you into an intimate relationship with God) can become a basis for your positive life message. It seems ironic that the things that hurt you and me and hold us back could eventually become the power in our life story.

> *With your help I can advance against a troop; with my God I can scale a wall.*
>
> (Psalm 18:29)

COMMON ROADBLOCKS TO GROWTH

Several different kinds of obstacles may prevent you from making proactive decisions that allow you to be your true self—and to do the "good works, which God prepared in advance" for you to do (Ephesians 2:10).

> *For God has not given us a spirit of fear and timidity, but of power, love, and self-discipline.*
>
> (2 Timothy 1:7, NLT)

Common Roadblocks to Intentional Living

Negative Self-Talk	Placating
Anger and Resentment	Perfectionism
Fear and Anxiety	Procrastination

4. Circle any of the obstacles in the above box that you think may be keeping you from doing what you—or God—want to do with your life. If you don't know how to respond right now, skip this exercise. You can come back to it later after reading the following stories and explanations.

Negative Self-Talk

Negative self-talk can thwart growth and keep you from maintaining healthy relationships with yourself and others. Anxiety levels increase with silent faulty statements such as, "Disappointing my parents would be terrible," or "If I make a mistake in front of others, it would be awful." The truth is, it might be distasteful, painful, annoying, inconvenient, even sad, but not the end of the world. Negative thought patterns usually fall into one of three categories:

- Absolutes, such as: "I must never be afraid of the future." Or "I will never be good enough."
- Personalization, such as: "When the boss criticizes a coworker, he is referring to my performance as well. I'd better shape up." Or "When my husband makes uncomplimentary remarks about the way another woman looks, he thinks the same about me."
- Overgeneralizations, such as: "This is how I am; I'll never change." Or "Men are always like that—I can't expect any better."

"What you think and believe determines how you feel and what you do,"[9] write William Backus and Marie Chapian in their book, *Telling Yourself the Truth*. Other negative self-talk examples include:

- I should keep all problems to myself.
- People must agree if they genuinely care about one another.
- Everyone else's needs and desires take priority over mine.

- My value depends on how well I spend each second of the day.
- Jesus expects me to give up all my right to privacy, rest, and recreation if I am to serve fully.

Growth will take place as you learn to change your negative self-talk into positive and realistic statements. For example, one of the above absolutes can be exchanged with the statement: Sometimes the unknown future scares me, but with God's help I'll gain courage to move through the fear.

As a young woman, I (Carol) was intrigued when others talked about their spiritual journal. Although I longed to start one, I told myself, "I don't write well. My life is not important enough to write about, anyway." I tried to push the idea out of my mind, but I wanted to know God better, and people assured me this would help.

I told myself I could try, although it might not work. I bought a book on journaling and a spiral notebook, and haltingly started writing down my prayers and thoughts. That was almost thirty years ago, and my journal has become a good friend. When I look back through these simple lined notebooks, I see how God has answered my prayers—giving me hope to trust Him for my current needs. If I had allowed my negative self-talk to keep me from journaling, I would have missed an effective method for personal and spiritual development—and a way for me to get to know God better.

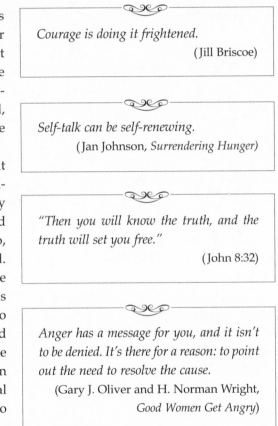

Courage is doing it frightened.
(Jill Briscoe)

Self-talk can be self-renewing.
(Jan Johnson, *Surrendering Hunger*)

"Then you will know the truth, and the truth will set you free."
(John 8:32)

Anger has a message for you, and it isn't to be denied. It's there for a reason: to point out the need to resolve the cause.
(Gary J. Oliver and H. Norman Wright, *Good Women Get Angry*)

ANGER AND RESENTMENT

Anger is a normal human response to a real or perceived wrong, inequity, or injustice. Yet I (Joan) believed that if I loved unselfishly I would never get angry. So I consistently refused to be upset. Of course I was angry when I was treated poorly, but I called it by another name, such as oversensitivity, and pushed it down.

Yet when anger is stuffed in the name of love and spirituality, it usually leads to resentment. Resentment left to seethe inside is self-destructive. Anger often signals a hidden hurt. Initially, to deal with my resentment, I chose to talk with a safe and caring person to release some of the hurt. Eventually I confronted the root of my anger. It took courage. God helped me to value the constructive role that an honest look at anger would have in my relationship with Him and others. He wanted me to be free from energy-draining resentment.

When I am afraid,
I will trust in you.
In God, whose word I praise,
in God I trust; I will not be afraid.
(Psalm 56:3-4)

FEAR AND ANXIETY

"Sometimes I get this strange sensation in my gut, like someone just slugged me," said Sally. "For years I didn't realize that my fear was causing it. Now I recognize that the pain surfaces when I feel someone disapproves of my behavior."

Sally has been conditioned to feel anxious. When she goes shopping and buys the wrong brands, her roommate responds, "how stupid." Even when they aren't together, she worries she'll make a mistake and her roommate will find out. When she makes a routine error at work, she worries she'll lose her job. Sally's fear of remaining single preoccupies her thoughts, and her constant concern of what other people think and say deprives her of joy and freedom.

God promises to deliver us from fear and torment, but that deliverance must be fueled by prayer, Scripture reading, faith in God, and obedience to Him.

(Thelma Wells, excerpted from *Women of Faith Study Bible*)

Fear robs you of feeling fully alive.
(Dennis E. O'Grady,
Taking the Fear Out of Change)

According to Carol Kent, author of the book, *Tame Your Fears*, there are five forms of "slavish" fear that women struggle with, including:

- Fear of things that haven't happened yet—phobias and potential disasters
- Fear of being vulnerable—losing control, failing, or revealing who I really am
- Fear of abandonment—worrying I will be rejected
- Fear of reality—perhaps I will not be able to handle the pain if I accept the truth
- Fear of making wrong choices—feeling trapped

Sally experienced less anxiety when she began to focus on her God-given strengths and allow faith to progressively replace her self-defeating fears.

5. What do you fear? (Perhaps you do not have any inappropriate fears—or as Carol Kent says, "slavish" fears. You do not need to make up a fear. Instead, contemplate what preoccupies your thoughts and drains your energy supply, threatening to short-circuit your personal, professional, and spiritual growth.)

Learn to accept yourself when you are feeling afraid.

(Dennis G. O'Grady,
Taking the Fear Out of Change)

There is a single second when faith becomes stronger than fear.

(Peg Rankin)

Surely you desire truth in the inner parts; you teach me wisdom in the inmost place.
(Psalm 51:6)

PLACATING

Years ago when I (Joan) attended one of Carol's Focus Forward seminars, she remarked to the group that some people "play to the grandstand instead of playing the game."

"I think that's what I've done," I responded silently. I visualized myself up to bat with the game tied in the ninth. *If I do this right, everyone will love and appreciate me.* In my daydream, as I searched the crowd for my family and friends' reaction, I consistently missed each pitch.

Then I realized that by concentrating primarily on others' responses to me I had thwarted God's efforts to coach me into becoming the life player He had in mind for me to be. I genuinely wanted to stop playing this placating game. This insight about myself gave me courage to move ahead—to better care for my health and adjust my excessive work schedule.

Fearing people is a dangerous trap.
(Proverbs 29:25, NLT)

PERFECTIONISM

Recently, I (Joan) talked with a friend who, like Carol and me, has struggled with the everything-must-be-just-right philosophy. She said, "I never claimed to be a perfectionist. Obviously, I don't look like one."

Perhaps you don't consider yourself to be a perfectionist because you have a messy closet or uncoordinated fashion accessories. However, perfectionism is subtler than that. It's related to unreasonable expectations, such as belittling yourself and others for having human (or weak) thoughts or emotions, inconsistent faith, or less-than-excellent accomplishments.

By learning not to be controlled by unrealistic expectations and refusing to react with panic to sudden unplanned circumstances, you can begin to relax. Your best at any given moment in any specific situation is what you have to offer. Your best may vary according to the unique conditions of each situation, but that's OK. You can admit the fear that your personal contributions to life might not be good enough. With God's help, you can move past perfectionistic panic to live in peace.

> *We all stumble in many ways. If anyone is never at fault in what he says, he is a perfect man.*
>
> (James 3:2)

> *Perfectionism is self-abuse of the highest order.*
>
> (Anne Wilson Shaef, *Meditations for Women Who Do Too Much*)

> *Not that I have already obtained all this, or have already been made perfect, but I press on to take hold of that for which Christ Jesus took hold of me.*
>
> (Philippians 3:12)

PROCRASTINATION

Covert perfectionism triggers procrastination. As a covert perfectionist you may not complete your education, pursue your dream job, or write the book you want to. You may not sing in the choir, buy a house, or risk making new friends because you're afraid of failing, appearing faulty, being shamed, or making a mistake. Eventually, making any decision may unnerve you, and procrastination becomes a habit. Fear of making a wrong choice or producing inferior work cancels any pleasure or pride you could have in your accomplishments.

Often our "I should" and "I ought to" thinking perpetuates this procrastination and perfectionism. It can make us afraid to take a risk and change. Passing through frightening and unfamiliar situations on the way to maturity is not always easy. When

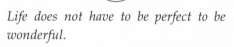

> *Life does not have to be perfect to be wonderful.*
>
> (Annette Funicello)

you are anxious (and you certainly will be at times) you can trust the One who is bigger than your fears.

Moving Beyond the Obstacles

Although you can decide to take proactive steps, you may require help moving beyond the obstacles to implement your decisions. At these times, you and I have a loving and powerful heavenly Father who is willing to do what we cannot see or figure out.

Yet faith in God can feel like the ultimate paradox. You release what you long for, let it go in order to find what's missing. This involves trusting that the decision to surrender is OK, the process will be worthwhile, and God is in complete control of the result.

> *Being confident of this, that he who began a good work in you will carry it on to completion until the day of Christ Jesus.*
>
> (Philippians 1:6)

Faith means loosening your grip on people, jobs, circumstances, expectations—and your capability to do it all just right. Faith is not resignation, but active release. There's a difference. Resignation brings defeat and joylessness; faith produces freedom and life.

6. Read the Hebrews verse printed here. What would it look like if you trusted God with all that you've learned about yourself—past, present and future—during this study?

> *It's impossible to please God apart from faith. And why? Because anyone who wants to approach God must believe both that he exists and that he cares enough to respond to those who seek him.*
>
> (Hebrews 11:6, MSG)

7. What obstacle keeps you from reaching your goals and serving God as you believe He wants you to do?

8. What resources or supports do you need to get past that obstacle at this time in your life?

9. Turn your responses to questions 6-8 into a prayer to God, jotting it down in this space.

> *Faith in God is the instrument which enables men and women to remove the hills of difficulty which block their path.*
>
> (William Barclay)

IW STORY: THERE'S POWER IN MY STORY

I always had a problem staying focused on what someone was saying. After a few minutes, I automatically tuned out. Yet no one knew this because I was a well-taught listener—able to look totally enthralled with what another was saying to me. Recently this became more annoying when I couldn't recall what I had been told. Also, I noticed that I had trouble "hearing" from God, although I wanted to. I could per- ceive His message to me through the study of His Word, but my mind raced to my next planned event when I tried to be quiet and sense God's message to me through my spirit. When I realized this was the same way I had been "listening" to others for years, I felt sad. I pleaded with the Lord to help me understand my problem. *Was there a personal development program I could take? A medicine that would help me?*

Then one morning during my routine run, I "heard" God's answer—not audibly, but deep down inside me. I understood why I had the listening problem. My mother had always lectured me. Dad only talked about himself. At an early age, I had learned to tune out. Yet I was never allowed to look like I was not listening. So while my body language assured that I had heard every word, instead I retreated into my own little world. It was my way of surviving the many lectures and monologues.

I have a new perspective now. God and I are working on my listening skills. I have come to appreciate my past because it has helped me come to know God better. I feel like I have walked hundreds of miles further in my journey with the Lord.

MARGARET SNYDER, BIBLE TEACHER

PART B:
WHAT IS MY NEXT ACTION STEP?

Change with a Purpose

"I thought I needed to make intentional decisions about what I would do *after* my son left for college," said Susan, a business owner from Minnesota. "Then it dawned on me: 'Why not make the most of these years... *before* he leaves?'"

How often have you said (aloud or silently), "When I finish school... " or "After I get married... " or "When the kids are all in school... " or "As soon as I get that promotion... " or "When I pay off the bills... " or "If my spouse would just shape up... " or "When my children are on their own... " *then* I'll get serious about making goals and following through?

Today is a gift from God, worth enjoying. Several years ago I (Joan) realized this truth and wrote the following words in my journal: *JCW, don't live in the future, always waiting, longing for what is not. Accept reality as a basis for continued growth. Stop fearing the present, wishing for different circumstances, dreaming of a future that may never be. Be intentional now.*

> *This is the day the LORD has made.*
> *let us rejoice and be glad in it.*
> (Psalm 118:24)

As a result of the questions, stories, and exercises in this book, you have learned:

- What is good about your life, what concerns you about your life, and what is lacking in your life right now

- How past experiences have helped shape you and how the people in your life have influenced you
- About your unique behavior characteristics and preferences
- About your realities and practicalities
- About your current opportunities and roles, stressors and supports
- About obstacles that can hold you back
- How commitment and faith in a loving and remarkable God can help you honor Him with the power of your life story

> *The most important source of motivation is not willpower but the power of a vision, an image of who God is calling us to be in Christ.*
>
> (Douglas Rumford, *Soul Shaping*)

NEXT ACTION STEP IDEAS

Determining your next step is not a one-time experience. Committing to follow through on your chosen goal is merely the next intentional step in a lifetime of purpose-full living. It is cooperating with God as He helps you live in harmony with the real you. You may want to choose another action step in six months or one year from now—or at your next life transition. But that's the future. What will be your next step for *now?* It may evolve from a need in any area of your life. Here's a list of some next step decisions from women in previous IW workshops.

- Develop a nutritional and exercise plan.
- Set up a household budget and stick to it.
- Get consultation help for menopausal symptoms.
- Start a plan to memorize Scripture each week.
- Find a prayer partner.
- Go back to school.
- Make an appointment with a counselor.
- Find a new service opportunity that utilizes my gifts.
- Say no to an activity that drains my energy and conflicts with my behavioral preferences.
- Set boundaries in an unhealthy relationship.
- Join a Bible study group.
- Finish writing a magazine article and submit it.
- Plan a nurturing date with myself each week—go to breakfast, attend a concert, meet a friend for coffee.
- Schedule a specific time on my calendar to spend with the Lord.

IW STORY: THE BLESSINGS OF INTENTIONALITY

While taking the Intentional Woman course, I realized I had a creative side that was underdeveloped and crying to be heard. Consequently, I signed up for a floral design class and thoroughly enjoyed it. This gave me courage to pursue my next creative adventure—a tap dance class. I registered for a class at the local community college.

Recently I performed with Tap Dance Arizona at a local Rehab Center. Prior to the performance, I had time to walk throughout the audience. I wanted to know the stories behind the faces, so I introduced myself and listened to their painful stories. Then I went back to my place behind the stage. When the curtain opened and I saw my new friends, I danced with new meaning. I felt I was a minister—bringing joy among sadness and hope amidst darkness.

At the same time, I volunteered as a crosswalk guard at the school. I dressed up in different costumes—one week as a clown, the next as a Disney character. The students loved it and so did the parents who drove by. Watching their smiles, my own soul was nourished.

Part of me wondered if it was selfish to pursue my creative dreams. Yet as I stepped out in faith, giving myself permission to be the person I was designed to be, God used my "fun" to minister to the people around me.

RAYNHAM HAUBER,
REGISTERED NURSE

IW STORY: INTENTIONAL STEP IN MY MARRIAGE

My husband's critical remarks were a part of everyday life. However, after he took early retirement, we were together most of the time. His remarks didn't make my adjustment to his retirement any easier. I decided I needed to address the way I responded to his criticism.

One day when he shot off a sharp put-down, I said, "I cannot accept what you have just said." After that incident every time he hurt me, I would let him know how I felt.

The intentional action step I took was the beginning of better communication between my husband and me—making our retirement years more enjoyable for both of us.

KAREN LARSON, PUBLISHED WRITER

IW STORY: PRAYING ON PAPER

I came to the Intentional Women seminar wondering what I should do next. In college I majored in music. Then I married my college sweetheart and became choir director at a church on the Mississippi River. One year later, we moved to Arizona and I began teaching music at an elementary school. I liked my role as music teacher, but I did not have assurance that I should continue.

Answering the questions and completing the exercises at the seminar was a learning experience for me. I made discoveries about myself and knew that it was up to me to decide what to do about what I had learned. My simple, yet intentional, next step was to start a journal. When I wrote down my thoughts and prayers, I began to understand what was really inside me.

In January I journaled, *God, if you are calling me to be a mother, let me know. I really can't figure this out.* By the end of February I wrote, *I have a yearning to be a mom. Is this from you, God?* In March someone asked about my teaching plans. I felt agitated and didn't know what to say. I poured out my confusion in my journal—becoming more comfortable listening to my heart and admitting my thoughts on paper.

I discovered I was pregnant in June. In my journal I wrote, *Thank You, Jesus, for this miracle living within me. This has been your process and you have prepared me.* I am glad I took the intentional step to start journaling, taking time to pray on paper—asking for God's guidance and opening up to His will in my life. I love my new role as mother to eighteen-month-old Max.

ANNE WEBB, MOTHER AND PART-TIME ADMINISTRATIVE ASSISTANT

YOUR NEXT INTENTIONAL STEP

Clarifying your next intentional step need not involve making a major life change, although it may. Perhaps for you it simply means taking a baby step within the context of your current circumstances. You don't have to do it all—just right—right now. Living intentionally is a lifetime process of getting to know your Creator and Savior better as He shows you more about who you are and what He has planned for you to do.

Take your everyday, ordinary life—your sleeping, eating, going-to-work, and walking-around life—and place it before God as an offering. Embracing what God does for you is the best thing you can do for him. . . . You'll be changed from the inside out. Readily recognize what he wants from you, and quickly respond to it. . . . God brings the best out of you, develops well-formed maturity in you.

(Romans 12:1-2, MSG)

Clarification Arrow

The Clarification Arrow is a reusable tool for choosing your next action step.

Pinpoint ➤ Pray ➤ Picture ➤ Plan ➤ Act

1. *Pinpoint* the intentional action you want to take at this time in your life. To do this, look again at your Wheel of Life (page 29), Roles Pinwheel (page 98), and Roles/Reality/Needs chart (page 117). You may wish to jot down several options before you decide which step to take. Has there been a theme threading through the answers you wrote? Is there a recurring thought or insight that keeps surfacing? If so, consider this when pinpointing what you want to do next.

2. *Pray* for wisdom, direction, and affirmation. Write out your prayer here.

3. *Picture* your desired outcome. What will it look like when you reach your goal?

❧ 4. *Plan* how you will accomplish your intention. What will you have to do to achieve your desired result? What resources do you need?

❧ 5. *Act* on your plan. What will you do? When will you do it? Who will you tell?

❧ 6. Which role or roles will this action step affect?

If you have the time and energy now, you may wish to follow the same pattern for each of the other roles in your life. Or you might make a date to do this at a later time.

> *Those who hear and don't act are like those who glance in the mirror, walk away, and two minutes later have no idea who they are, what they look like.*
>
> *But whoever catches a glimpse of the revealed counsel of God — the free life! — even out of the corner of his eye, and sticks with it, is no distracted scatterbrain but a . . . woman of action. That person will find delight and affirmation in the action.*
>
> (James 1:22-25, MSG)

Cultivating Supportive Relationships

You need encouragement and accountability in order to stay committed to an action step. God didn't plan for you to grow or develop in isolation. We really do need each other's support.

> *Therefore encourage one another and build each other up, just as in fact you are doing.*
>
> (1 Thessalonians 5:11)

IW STORY: MY BUDDY SYSTEM

I've been fighting battles since childhood. Sometimes I think I could challenge Xena, television's Warrior Princess. My parents divorced when I was fourteen years old, and I took on a mother role, caring for my mom and sister. I acted no-nonsense, capable, and self-assured, but on the inside I was insecure and afraid.

In adulthood, I continued to fight—for my marriage as we went through difficult times and for my two teenagers when they faced struggles inherent in children diagnosed with mood disorders. For their sake, I took on teachers, administrators, counselors, and doctors. Because I usually kept fighting until the adversary was worn down, I often won.

As a believer in Jesus, I often prayed for God's help and wisdom to fight my battles. *Then why did I always feel tired, like I was carrying a refrigerator on my back?*

Recently, while meeting with a group of friends, I broke down and cried, confessing my exhaustion. After praying for me, one woman said, "Diane, the battle is not yours to fight! Read 2 Chronicles 20:17. You don't have to struggle alone." Her words and my friends' prayers encourage me when I'm tempted to play the Warrior Princess role again. I know I need their reassurance and support.

DIANE MARKINS,
MARKETING CONSULTANT AND WRITER

> *But you will not even need to fight. Take your positions; then stand still and watch the LORD's victory.*
>
> (2 Chronicles 20:17, NLT)

7. Think about a time in your life when you were in transition or faced significant change or decisions. Who supported you? What did they do or say that helped you?

8. What kind of support do you need to follow through on your action step(s)?

*P*ART *E*:
USE MY STORY FOR YOUR GLORY, LORD.

Revisiting the Key Reason for Living Intentionally

In the first section of this book, you read the key reason for living intentionally: to glorify God as the person He designed you to be. I (Carol) shared with you what it means to me: accepting my uniqueness—the way God created me—and pulling out all the stops to develop my gifts and use them purposefully to serve God.

> *Now to him who is able to do immeasurably more than all we ask or imagine, according to his power that is at work within us, to him be glory.*
>
> (Ephesians 3:20-21)

CAROL'S CURRENT ACTION STEP
Recently while using the Clarification Arrow and working through the Pinpoint, Pray, Picture, Plan, and Act process, I pinpointed a next action step in my role as a LifePlan facilitator. Although I enjoy the two-day individualized interaction I have with women and will continue to book LifePlans, I long to make this process available to more women. I am praying about ways to maximize my time and energy at this season of my life so I can continue to empower women to live on-purpose lives.

I picture godly women leaders guiding other women from their churches and communities through the five-step Intentional Woman process. I envision women being released from what holds them back and becoming excited about glorifying God with their lives. I want to train these godly women leaders and work with them to try new

> *We can be mirrors that brightly reflect the glory of the Lord. And as the Spirit of the Lord works within us, we become more and more like him and reflect his glory even more.*
>
> (2 Corinthians 3:18, NLT)

approaches for group facilitation. I will develop a written strategy for implementing this idea by the first of next year. Who will I tell? My prayer partners. I will be accountable to Joan.

JOAN'S CURRENT ACTION STEP

Since moving to Arizona three years ago, I have focused on working and meeting deadlines. Although I'm grateful for the opportunities I've had to pursue several lifetime dreams, I feel like my soul needs replenishing. Consequently, I have pinpointed an action step for my Self-Care Manager role: I will locate a silent retreat center in the Phoenix area and go there for two nights. Then I'll schedule an overnight retreat quarterly for the next year.

I will pray that God will refresh my body, mind, soul, and spirit. As an introvert, I gain strength from being alone, so I picture that my inner motor will slow down and I'll be more content with the accomplishments of a relaxed Joan Webb. In order to fulfill this goal, I need to make telephone calls to find a retreat, schedule a getaway time, work it out with my family and employer, find transportation, pack, and go. When will I do this? I will schedule the first retreat for sometime next month. Who will I tell and be accountable to? Carol.

IW STORY: "MY LIFE" IS SAFE WITH GOD

I placed "my life" on top of the car—all the pages of answered questions and completed exercises from the Intentional Woman process. Then I juggled my books, Bible, and purse while I dug for my keys. Relieved that I found them, I stashed my bag and books inside the car and drove off to do errands and attend another meeting.

Driving home hours later, it occurred to me that I was missing my "life papers." Frantically I scanned the interior of the car. My heart pounded in my throat and my stomach tightened. I knew without a doubt I had left "my life" on the top of the car in that parking lot and had driven off.

Because I was honest and wrote all kinds of personal things about my past, present, and future, I was terrified—anyone or everyone could see it all. *How could I have been so stupid, careless, dumb?*

Once I reached our house, I raced past my husband to get to the telephone, yelling that I had done something terribly stupid and he wouldn't believe it. "What have you done?" he asked.

"Sshhuusshh," I whispered, frantically dialing the church's number. While I waited for someone to answer, my husband tried to ascertain what was wrong. "You wrecked the car?" No. "The police stopped you?" No. "You hit someone?" "No, no," I replied. "This is much worse. My 'life' is revealed for the world to see—

or at least the people in the church who all know me."

Finally the receptionist answered and promised she would send someone to look in the parking lot and then call me back. I could not relax. I moaned and prayed it would be found. My husband couldn't believe my anguish. "Is that all?" he said. But I felt naked, vulnerable, exposed to the world.

Then the telephone rang and I learned it had been found and would be kept safe until I could retrieve it. The next day, when I picked it up, I was surprised that nothing was missing and everything was still in pristine condition. *Thank You, Lord,* I murmured.

That's when I heard it—that inaudible voice inside me: *Audrey, I can take care of your life. No one will run over it without My say-so. It will not be revealed for the world to see unless I allow it. If you lose your life, I will give it back to you. Don't be afraid anymore, because I am with you—always. And one more thing: I would never call you dumb, stupid, or idiotic when you make a mistake. I love you.* I believe God tailor-made this experience to reassure me to trust Him with my life—past, present, and future.

AUDREY THORKELSON, LEADERSHIP TRAINER

I'm Trusting You, Lord

1. Spend a few moments in silent conversation with God. Perhaps you would like to use the following sentence-starters as a prayer guide.

Lord, I praise You because . . .

Thank You for helping me understand . . .

Please give me wisdom to . . .

And the courage to . . .

I acknowledge that the desire of my heart is . . .

Continue in Your process of showing me who I am now and who I can become, the woman You had in mind when You created me. I'm trusting You, Lord. Please use my life story for Your glory. In Jesus' name, Amen.

 2. After having completed this Intentional Woman five-step process, what acknowledgment, affirmation, or encouragement would you like to give yourself?

> *Life is a ribbon. What are you tying, knots or bows?*
>
> (Patsy Clairmont, *Extravagant Grace*)

Our Privilege as Intentional Women

Every day we live gains us a new yesterday of experience to incorporate into our maturing process. One day at a time is how a new positive behavior becomes a habit. If we try to tackle all the days at once, we become overwhelmed. But by taking one step at a time, we will have a lifetime of intentional living. And by daily committing all that we are (and know) to God's loving care, allowing His Spirit to guide, we will experience a lifetime of glorifying God.

> *For we are God's masterpiece. He has created us anew in Christ Jesus, so that we can do the good things he planned for us long ago.*
>
> (Ephesians 2:10, NLT)

We have discovered that becoming the intentional women God created us to be leads to the good things He planned for us to do. This is how we have experienced the power of our life stories and the privilege and thrill of partnering with God.

We feel as though God has entwined our hearts with yours. We have prayed for you, our readers, and will continue to do so. Our hope is that we can continue to encourage each other to appreciate God's loving-kindness in producing our unique life stories. Together, may we grow to love Him more and find delight in living intentionally in every season of our lives.

For Groups

Guidelines for Facilitation

Purpose of Workbook

This workbook is a discovery guide combining both Bible study and personal growth exercises. It is designed to guide a woman through a five-step process that will:

- help her appreciate her life story and discover and utilize its unique power
- help her recognize God's goodness and love in developing her story
- empower her to live a life of purpose and meaning
- help her develop a next step action plan for living intentionally right now

Tips for Facilitators

For maximum effectiveness we suggest that group leaders:

- read the workbook and complete all questions and exercises before facilitating a group.
- share the process with at least one other person before leading a group through the five-step process.
- provide a caring and safe environment for women to share their honest thoughts and feelings.
- facilitate dialogue that results as the women's stories unfold; you will not be teaching information.
- model active listening skills as information and insights are disclosed during the group discussion times.
- remember that group participants will continue to work through what they have learned long after the last session, so they do not need to be rushed to find solutions.
- encourage everyone to answer briefly, rather than just two or three women answering at length. Tactfully cut short lengthy stories.

Format Suggestions

A six-week study means you will cover one step per week using the Prep Steps for the opening session. If you choose this format, the participants can obtain the workbooks ahead of time. Alternatively, you can guide them through the Prep Steps in the first session, allowing silent time for them to respond to the questions and calling them back to the group (or sub-group) to share. In the six-week format, the exercises for steps one through five should be completed before class. During the ninety-minute session, the women will share their responses and insights. (If possible, you might want to consider leading a two-hour weekly session to allow for more relaxed interaction.) Homework will take 1-1½ hours each week.

After a ten-to-fifteen-minute opening time that includes the prayer and introduction, use your discretion to assign the time given to each exercise. For each week's ninety-minute session, you might consider assigning twenty-five minutes to each part (A, B, and C).

Another option is to cover the workbook in twelve rather than six sessions. In this format, each step will take two sessions to complete. Women can complete the questions and exercises for each session at home in about forty-five minutes.

These facilitator notes are written for the six-week format. If you use a different time frame, adapt the suggestions to fit your needs.

Suggested Ground Rules

Review these guidelines with the group during your first session.

- *Maintain confidentiality.* No one should repeat what someone shares in the group unless given express permission. Even then, discretion is imperative.
- *Emphasize attendance.* Each session builds on the previous one. Ask group members to be on time and to commit to attending all six sessions, unless an emergency arises.
- *Encourage participation.* It is important that each person participate in some way. However, assure the women that they may "pass" if they do not want to answer a specific question. Tell the participants that there are no right or wrong answers— only *their* answers.
- *Offer prayer.* Open and close each session with prayer. Ask group members to pray for you as the facilitator and for one another. Pray that the women will accept one another, respond honestly, and be open to learning and growing.
- *Enjoy your time together.* Be gentle with yourself (as facilitator) and with the group members. There is no perfect formula for a successful group.

SESSION ONE

Prep Steps

Key Objective: *To become comfortable with what to expect as you work through this five-step process and to understand why it is important to live intentionally.*

The atmosphere of the first session sets the tone for the following sessions. Your chief tasks for this meeting are to help the women relax and get to know one another, and to help them understand what to expect in the upcoming sessions. Always start on time. Assign someone to welcome and assist latecomers.

- COMING-TOGETHER ACTIVITY: Ask each woman to find something in her purse or wallet that represents a facet of her life, hold it up, and then tell the group about it. For example, she might have the program from a band concert in her purse, so she could tell about her son who plays the tuba. As facilitator, you should begin the sharing. Keep your comments brief and lighthearted.

- OPENING PRAYER: Open with prayer.

- INTRODUCE THE WORKBOOK: Give a brief testimony about your experience in completing the Intentional Woman process. Share what excites you about leading the group. Go over the suggested group guidelines and discuss the option of having prayer partners. These partners need not meet together outside the group session time, but they could share requests during the week by phone or e-mail. You might draw numbers to determine partners.

- INTRODUCE THE KEY OBJECTIVE AND KEY VERSE FOR THE FIRST SESSION.

- PART A: HOW CAN I DISCOVER THE POWER OF MY LIFE STORY? If this session is the first time the women have seen *The Intentional Woman*, have participants share the responsibility for reading aloud the Prep Step sections. Allow three to four quiet minutes for them to respond to questions 1 and 2, and then have them briefly share their written responses.

- PART B: WHAT *IS* INTENTIONAL LIVING, ANYWAY? Share reading responsibilities again. As facilitator, you will lead the John 21:17-21 Bible study. Then ask several women to read the benefits of intentional living. Allow quiet time to complete questions 3 to 6. Ask the women to share their responses to questions 7 and 8. You might wish to share first as an example.

- CLOSING: Before the ending prayer, encourage the women to begin the homework early in the week so they'll have enough time to reflect on the questions for the next step.

Session Two

Step One: Come As You Are Today

> **Key Objective:** *To determine your current situation (reality/needs/desires) and clarify your quest.*

Always start on time. Assign someone to welcome and assist latecomers.

- COMING-TOGETHER ACTIVITY: Ask the following question: What impressed you from your reading last week? (If your group has more than eight members, everyone may not have time to respond.)

- OPENING PRAYER.

- INTRODUCE THE KEY OBJECTIVE AND KEY VERSE.

- PART A: WHERE AM I RIGHT NOW? Ask several women to share how they rewrote Psalm 32:8 (question 1).

- WHEEL OF LIFE EXERCISE: Refer to the Wheel of Life exercise, and ask the women to share their responses to question 5.

- PART B: WHAT IS GOING ON IN MY LIFE? Divide the women into pairs or triads to share their answers to the three questions.

- PART C: HERE I AM, LORD. Ask participants to share the verses they chose for their prayers and why.

- CLOSING: Before the ending prayer, encourage the women to begin the homework early in the week so they'll have sufficient time to remember past experiences.

Session Three

Step Two: Celebrate Your Yesterdays

> **Key Objective:** *To reflect on and celebrate your life, looking for strengths developed through past opportunities and adversity.*

Always start on time. Assign someone to welcome and assist latecomers.

- COMING TOGETHER ACTIVITY: Ask the following question: What impressed you from your reading last week?

- OPENING PRAYER.

- INTRODUCE THE KEY OBJECTIVE AND KEY VERSE.

- PART A: THERE'S POWER IN *MY* STORY? Discuss group members' responses to questions 1 and 2.

- PART B: WHERE HAVE I BEEN? Ask the women to divide into pairs and briefly share their responses to one of the questions in this part.

- PART C: THIS IS WHAT I SEE, LORD. Focus on question 4. According to the available time, feedback can be given in the whole group or in subgroups.

- CLOSING: Before the ending prayer, you may want to briefly explain the Pace/Priority survey participants will complete during the coming week. You may base your comments on your own experience completing the survey.

Session Four
Step Three: Commit It All to God

> **Key Objective:** *To sense in a fresh way how much God wants to have an intimate and growing relationship with you. To believe He longs to help you understand yourself and commit your life (including your future) to His wise and loving care.*

- COMING TOGETHER ACTIVITY: Ask the following question: What impressed you from your reading last week?

- OPENING PRAYER.

- INTRODUCE THE KEY OBJECTIVE AND KEY VERSE.

- PART A: DO YOU LIKE ME, LORD? Discuss participants' responses to question 2. Limit the time spent on Part A to allow more discussion for Part B.

- PART B: WHAT AM I DISCOVERING ABOUT GOD'S DESIGN FOR ME? Divide into pairs or triads according to your DISC behavior styles. For example, all D's will be together, all I's together, and so on. If you have only one person who represents one of the styles, she can team up with two others. Discuss questions 7 and 8.

- PART C: I SURRENDER, LORD. Read aloud The Turning Point section and have women discuss the topic of surrender. Then provide a quiet time for each woman to reflect on her prayer response. (Optional: Allow time for a few women to share their commitment response.)

- CLOSING: Before the ending prayer, suggest that the women may want to share their response to Part C with their prayer partner sometime during the next week.

SESSION FIVE
Step Four: Consider Your Choices

> **Key Objective:** *To look at how your God-given uniqueness—and your past and present experiences—work together to help you make wise and intentional choices about your future.*

- COMING TOGETHER ACTIVITY: Ask the following question: What impressed you from your reading last week?

- OPENING PRAYER.

- INTRODUCE THE KEY OBJECTIVE AND KEY VERSE.

- PART A: WHAT ARE MY OPPORTUNITIES? Lead a brainstorming session modeled after question 1, recording responses on a flip chart or white board. Limit time spent on Part A to allow more discussion on the Roles Pinwheel.

- PART B: WHAT ARE MY CURRENT ROLES? Divide into pairs or triads and discuss the Roles Pinwheel, focusing on questions 5 and 6.

- PART C: I WANT TO MAKE WISE CHOICES, LORD. Ask women to share a reality and/or practicality about their season and one exciting activity from question 3.

- CLOSING: Before the ending prayer, remind participants that the next session is the last one. Encourage them to start their homework early so they have sufficient time to clarify their next action step.

SESSION SIX
Step Five: Clarify Your Next Steps

> **Key Objective:** *To clarify your next action step so you can take responsibility for your growth and your use of time and energy.*

- COMING TOGETHER ACTIVITY: Ask the following question: What impressed you from your reading last week?

- OPENING PRAYER.

- INTRODUCE THE KEY OBJECTIVE AND KEY VERSE.

- PART A: WHAT WILL IT TAKE TO GROW? Have each woman share one role from the chart on exercise 2. Then discuss the obstacles to growth and question 8.

- PART B: WHAT IS MY NEXT ACTION STEP? Divide into pairs or triads, and share your responses to questions 1 and 5. If you have time, answer question 8.

- PART C: USE MY STORY FOR YOUR GLORY, LORD. In your large group, invite women to share their responses to question 2.

- CLOSING: Form a circle, holding hands. Ask each woman to pray silently or aloud for the woman on her right. When others are finished, close in prayer.

Notes

1. Creative Memories, August 25, 2001, http://www.creativememories.com/philmiss.asp.

2. Joan C. Webb, Adapted from *Meditations for Christians Who Try To Be Perfect* (SanFrancisco: Harper, 1993) (out of print), p. 284.

3. Charles F. Boyd, *Different Children, Different Needs* (Sisters, Oreg.: Multnomah, 1994), p. 39.

4. Boyd, p. 48.

5. Stephen Arterburn and Dave Stoop, *Seven Keys to Spiritual Renewal* (Wheaton: Tyndale, 1998), p. 21.

6. Carol Van Klompenburg, *What to Do When You Can't Do It All* (Minneapolis, Minn.: Augsburg, 1989), pp. 65-66.

7. Tom Paterson, *Living the Life You Were Meant to Live* (Nashville, Tenn.: Thomas Nelson, 1998), p. 76.

8. Jan Johnson, *Living a Purpose-Full Life*, (Colorado Springs, Colo.: WaterBrook, 1999), p. 200.

9. William Backus and Marie Chapian, *Telling Yourself the Truth* (Minneapolis, Minn.: Bethany House, 1980), p. 22.

Authors

CAROL TRAVILLA, a certified LifePlan facilitator, has a deep passion to help women discover and clarify their purpose in life. Author of the workbook *Caring Without Wearing,* Carol has developed curriculum and facilitated classes on personal and spiritual growth. She has a B.A. in Christian education and an M.A. in counseling psychology. Carol and her husband, Ken, currently live in Tempe, Arizona, where they minister at Grace Community Church. They have two married children and four lively grandsons.

JOAN C. WEBB is presently a freelance writer and the Family to Family international director for Venture International, a Christian relief and development agency with projects in the Middle East and Central Asia. The author of seven books, Joan teaches writing and personal growth workshops. Her book credits include the four-book series *Devotions for Little Boys and Girls,* and study notes for four Old Testament books in the *Women of Faith Study Bible.* Joan and her husband, Richard, live in Arizona. They have two children and two grandchildren.

FIND MEANING AND PURPOSE THAT LASTS.

Choosing Rest

One of God's greatest gifts to us—rest—is also one of the most elusive. But Jesus wants to give us His rest right now, in the midst of our restlessness of heart. *Choosing Rest* will show you how to claim this amazing gift.
(Sally Breedlove)

Holy Habits

This book will challenge you to live purposefully, regard each day with an eternal perspective, and allow God's character to impact your life in such a way that you reflect Him.
(Mimi Wilson and Shelly Cook Volkhardt)

Becoming a Woman of Influence

Do you seek deep, connective relationships that will encourage you to grow? Discover principles for building solid relationships through simple steps to mentoring.
(Carol Kent)

To get your copies, visit your local bookstore, call 1-800-366-7788, or log on to www.navpress.com. Ask for a FREE catalog of NavPress products. Offer #BPA.

NAVPRESS
BRINGING TRUTH TO LIFE
www.navpress.com